Beautiful Designs
with SuperDuos and Twin Beads

CAROLYN CAVE

KALMBACH BOOKS

Kalmbach Books
21027 Crossroads Circle
Waukesha, Wisconsin 53186
www.Kalmbach.com/Books

Published in 2014
18 17 16 15 14   1 2 3 4 5

Manufactured in the United States of America

ISBN: 978-1-62700-054-3
EISBN: 978-1-62700-055-0

Editor: Erica Swanson
Book Design: Carole Ross
Photographers: William Zuback, James Forbes

Library of Congress Control Number: 2014950467

Contents

Introduction 4
About Twin Beads and SuperDuos. 5
Tools and Materials 6
Techniques. 8

Bracelets
Duet – *twin peyote stitch* 17
City Lights – *twin square stitch* 19
Nine Patch – *twin right-angle weave*. 22
Snowberry – *twin St. Petersburg chain* 25
Warp Speed – *basket weave stitch*. 28
Liberty – *modified circular netting*. 31
Aleksandra – *Russian spiral* 34

Rings and Earrings
Europa – *circular netting* 38
Dahlia – *stitching twins with the hole facing up*. 41
Khione – *two-needle stitching* 44
Prairie Spring – *dual layer circular netting* 46
Erica – *circular netting beaded bead* 49
De Vine – *vertical ladder stitch* 51

Ropes
Gilana – *modified stringing* .55
Mossy River – *tubular peyote* 57
Viking's Double – *twin tubular herringbone*. 60
Theodora – *tubular herringbone with twin accents* 62

Chains and Pendants
Delft Lace – *two-needle stitching* 66
Twin Helix – *spiral vertical ladder*. 69
Marrakesh – *spiral stitch* 72
Seeing Double – *circular herringbone* 76
Midnight Sky – *capture a cabochon (beaded)* 78
Loretta – *setting a rivoli, two-needle stitching*. 82
Once in a Blue Moon – *capture a cabochon (sewn)* 85

Specialty Jewelry
Andante – *tubular peyote beaded beads, stringing* 90
Candy Chain – *curved vertical ladder*. 92
Oriana – *peyote fans* 95
Elsie – *peyote stitch* 99
Winter Harvest – *wheat stitch, stringing*. 104

Gallery 108
Acknowledgments 111
Artist Biography 111

Introduction

Two-hole beads have captured the design imaginations of the beading community, more than doubling (so to speak!) creative potential with their unique shape. Beaders can now make designs not otherwise possible!

Inside this book, you will find a wide variety of jewelry designs featuring twin beads and SuperDuo beads. You will also find a section outlining various stitches using twin beads; you will learn how they are similar to stitches made with single-hole beads, and how they differ. There are even several new stitches for you to try that are only possible with two-hole beads.

Once you have mastered the basic stitches, it's time to try your hand at making some bracelets. Then there are rings to make, both for the ears and the finger. Tubular versions of two-hole bead stitches are explored in a chapter on beaded ropes. From there the book will take you to more complex designs featuring intricate chains and pendants. Lastly is a chapter on elegant jewelry to stitch that will elevate the humble two-hole bead to designer status.

Creativity has always been a part of my life. I have explored many aspects of arts and crafts, from cross-stitch to crochet, sewing to spinning, knitting to needlecrafts, fabric dyeing to photography. Even in my formal education as a musician and as a performer, I have enjoyed many opportunities to be creative. I liked making other designers' projects, but I have discovered that designing my own jewelry is very rewarding. In the last few years, a whole book's worth of projects started to take shape. One idea led to more, and soon ideas for another book emerged. This is the book you're holding.

It has been immensely satisfying to explore a small percentage of two-hole bead design possibilities within the covers of this book, and I hope you will want to stitch some of them! Perhaps it will inspire you to create some of your own designs.

I create what I love, and I love what I create. I am thankful for having been given this opportunity to create projects for these pages. I hope that you will enjoy stitching them as much as I have enjoyed making them for you.

There are no mistakes when you create, only possibilities.

About Twin Beads and SuperDuos

Two-hole seed beads known as "twins" and "SuperDuos" came into the beading world near the end of 2011. They are made in the Czech Republic by companies that have manufactured beads for hundreds of years. These rice-shaped beads are 5mm long, 2.5mm thick, and were originally made in 80 colors. More colors have been produced over the years, and now there are over 300 shades and finishes to choose from.

There are some differences between twins and SuperDuos.

Twin beads are made by the same method as traditional seed beads. The glass is drawn into long threads, cut into lengths and then tumbled to finish and polish. This process means that the beads are consistent but not exactly uniform in shape and size. The glass is either clear or black, and then various colors and finishes are added to the surface. Occasionally one of the holes may be blocked, and the finish may possibly wear off over time. There are about 18 twin beads per gram.

The ends of SuperDuo beads are more pinched than a twin, and they are slightly fatter in the middle.

Projects may be affected by this difference. During the manufacturing process, the glass is pressed into a mold. This means that the beads are uniform in size and shape. The color of the bead's glass is consistent throughout the bead. The beads are little heavier than twins so you will get about 15 beads per gram. Because they are more uniform in quality, they are often a bit more expensive. The colors tend to be specialized, and have unique finishes, like picasso and AB coatings.

Projects in this book have been made with twin beads and SuperDuos. If both beads are mentioned in the materials list, you can choose which bead you would prefer to use. If only one is mentioned, the project is better suited to the type of bead stated. When slightly uneven twin beads are used, the project will have a more organic feel. If you prefer an orderly look, SuperDuos are more suitable.

twin bead

SuperDuo

Tools and Materials

Basic Tool Kit
Every project in this book requires:
- beading needles
- sharp scissors
- 2 pairs of chainnose or bentnose pliers
- ruler or tape measure
- Fireline beading thread, 8 or 10 lb. test, crystal or smoke

Extra tools will be listed in projects as needed.

Needles
The size number of beading needles decreases as the needle's diameter increases; size 10 needles are thicker than size 12. Size 10 is suitable for most beadwork. Size 12 is needed for very small beads or for multiple passes through a single bead.

Thread and Stringing Material
The type of beadwork you are doing determines the thread or stringing material used. For bead stitching, there are many choices of beading thread. These come in a wide variety of colors to suit most projects. Your choice should be based on the flexibility that is needed and the durability of the thread to suit the type of project. Synthetic fiber is more durable than natural. Beads are made of glass and glass is sharp. If your project is meant to be worn every day,

make sure the thread is strong. If your project gets occasional wear, the thread can be less durable. Don't choose thread that will disintegrate over time. If you put the effort into making beautiful jewelry, it needs to last!

If your beading thread won't easily go through your needle, give the end of it a pinch with a pair of pliers.

Work Surface
The area that you work in should have good light, either natural or from a lamp with a daylight spectrum bulb in it. You don't want your beads to skitter away, so use a fabric beading mat (for example, Vellux). Make sure the area you work in is uncluttered and free of items that can snag a working thread.

Lay the beads for each project in small piles or containers on your work surface. Label each to match the instructions, if necessary.

I keep a small piece of wood on my desk. It is useful for anchoring a pin, pushing a needle, or using as a surface to undo a stubborn knot.

Scissors
Use a pair of sharp scissors with a point that snips thread close to your work.

Measurements
My preferred ruler is metal, which is very accurate. I also use a small retractable tape measure, to measure longer distances around curves. Your

rulers should have both metric and imperial measurements on them since both are used for beading.

"Undo" Tool

We all make mistakes and have to unpick our work. I keep a few sizes of thick darning needles nearby and use them to undo threads when I have to. I don't recommend a sewing stitch ripper. It usually has a blade in it and you may accidentally cut your thread.

Pliers

There are various types of pliers, all used for grasping and holding. Only three are used in this book:

Chainnose pliers have a flat blade and a narrow tip.

Bentnose pliers are like chainnose pliers but have a bent tip. I prefer these, and use them for opening jump rings and ear wires, and to gently pull my needle through tight spaces.

Roundnose pliers have round blades, which become gradually smaller towards the tip. They are essential for making uniform plain or wrapped loops.

Sketch Book, Notepad, Paper, Pencil, Colored Pencils

If you would like to make changes to designs in this book, or become interested in making some designs of your own, paper and a pencil become essential tools.

Sketch and write down what changes you would like to make. Cut pictures that inspire you out of magazines, brochures, and catalogs.

Paste them into a scrapbook. Write down ideas that pop into your head. Draw a sketch of what you would like to design. Draw a simple diagram of an idea you saw elsewhere. The drawings do not have to be precise or look like da Vinci drew them. They are for your reference, and only you have to see them. Sketches are a way to trigger your memory of what you were thinking about at the time. You may like to add color to your sketches, particularly if you see a combination of shades that captures your attention.

Techniques

Sewing beads together with needle and thread follow specific patterns and commonly-used stitches. Introducing beads with two holes means that some changes need to be made. This can happen in two ways—the stitches can be done in the same way, which means the pattern may not look at all similar to the single-hole version; or, the stitches can be done so that the pattern looks the same as the single-hole version. This section offers instructions for some of the more common stitches using SuperDuos and twin beads. Later, you will explore projects made with some of these stitches.

Peyote Stitch

Peyote is a common stitch in both modern and traditional beadwork. It makes a dense fabric of beads resembling bricks, one row of beads offset to the next row. Unlike bricks, which are laid down in horizontal rows, the beads are stitched in vertical columns, often referred to as rows.

Even Count

Pick up an even number of twins. This makes the first two rows.
Row 3: Pick up a twin and sew through the second hole of the second-to-last twin picked up. Pick up one twin. Skip a twin in the previous row and sew through the second hole of the next twin. The first row of twins should flip over and begin to form a brick-like pattern. Repeat to the end (**figure 1**).
Row 4: Pick up a twin, skip a twin, and sew through the second hole of the next protruding twin. Repeat to the end of the row (**figure 2**).

Figure 1

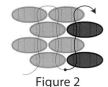

Figure 2

Odd Count

This stitch is executed exactly like even-count peyote but the row begins by picking up an odd number of twins (**figures 3 and 4**). The ends of the rows will have either an odd number of protruding beads, or an even number, depending on the number of rows stitched (**figures 5 and 6**).

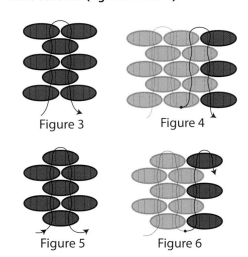

Figure 3   Figure 4

Figure 5   Figure 6

Horizontal Ladder Stitch

Horizontal ladder stitch is often used as the base for other stitches. It can be done with one needle or two. I prefer two because it provides a more even tension.

One Needle

Pick up a twin (this is the first hole) and sew through the second hole. Pick up another twin. Sew back through the second hole of the previous twin and the first hole of the new twin. Sew through the second hole of the new twin. Repeat, adding beads as you go. The thread loop between the two twins will always circle in the same direction (**figure 1**).

 Figure 1

Two Needles

Attach a needle to each end of a length of thread. Pick up a twin and sew through the second hole. With the other needle, sew through the second hole from the opposite direction so the threads cross inside the hole. Center this bead on the thread. With one needle, pick up a second twin. With the other needle, sew through the same hole from the opposite direction so the threads cross inside the hole. Cross the threads through the second hole. Repeat **(figure 2)**.

 Figure 2

One Needle, Stabilized

Because twins are rounded, they do not sit end-to-end very well. To work around this problem, add an 11º or 15º seed bead to sit between each twin. Using a single needle, pick up a twin and sew through the second hole. Pick up a seed bead, a twin, and a seed bead. Sew through the second hole of the twin, the seed bead, and the first hole of the second twin. Sew through the second hole of the twin. Repeat **(figure 3)**.

 Figure 3

Two Needles, Stabilized

Pick up a twin. Cross the threads through the second hole and center the twin on the thread. Pick up a seed bead with one needle, and a seed bead and a twin with the second needle. Cross the threads through the first hole of the twin. Cross the threads through the second hole. Repeat **(figure 4)**.

 Figure 4

Vertical Ladder Stitch

Vertical ladder stitch is unique to twins. I found that I used this stitch regularly so it has earned a name and place in this section.

Pick up an alternating pattern of a twin with a seed bead (10º or smaller works best), ending with a twin. Turn around by sewing through the second hole of the twin. Sew through the second hole of each twin, adding a seed bead between each **(figure)**.

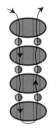

Herringbone Stitch

The pairs of beads in each row of this stitch lean slightly and resemble stockinette stitch in knitting. You can either use the traditional technique with twins and seed beads for a new (less angled) look—or you can modify the traditional technique to achieve the look of herringbone with twins.

Traditional Technique, New Look

Row 1: Make a twin horizontal ladder using the desired number of beads.

Row 2: Pick up two seed beads (10º or 11º). Sew down through the second hole and up through the next hole. Repeat to the end of the row, sewing down through the last hole. Sew around the outside of the last twin and up through the last seed bead added **(figure 1)**. The ladder stitch row

Figure 1

can be omitted. However, the work will not sit straight until the second row has been added.

Row 3: Pick up a twin and two seed beads. Sew through the second hole and down through the seed bead of the previous row. Sew up through the next seed bead. Repeat to the end of the row, sewing down through the last seed bead. Sew around the outside of the last seed bead, up through the last hole of the twin and the seed bead above it **(figure 2)**.

Figure 2

New Technique, Traditional Look
To achieve the knitted fabric herringbone look with twins, an entirely different approach is needed. Cut a long length of thread and attach needles to each end.

Row 1: With one needle, pick up an alternating pattern of two twins and two seed beads, ending with two twins. Center all of the beads on the thread. With each needle, sew through the second hole of the twin at the end of the row.

Row 2: With one needle, pick up two twins. Sew through the second hole of the next two twins in the row below. Repeat to the end of the row. With the other needle, follow the thread path back along the row. With each needle, pick up three seed beads and sew through the second hole of the twin at the end of the row **(figure 3)**. It is possible to do this stitch

Figure 3

with one needle and a single thread. However, this means that the ends of the rows will not have a symmetrical finish.

Square Stitch

Square stitch is effectively a series of vertical ladders joined together. Done with twins, it offers a challenge since the rounded beads do not nestle together well. Because of this, extra beads need to be used.

Make a vertical ladder using as many twins as needed. Use a turn-around stitch to secure the end of the row: sew back through the first bead and up again through its second hole **(figure 1)**.

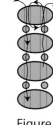

Figure 1

Row 2: Pick up a twin. Connect it to the twin beside using horizontal ladder stitch. Pick up a seed bead and a twin. Connect it to the twin in the row beside using horizontal ladder stitch **(figure 2)**. Repeat to the end of the row. Turn around by sewing through the second hole of the last twin picked up. Sew back through all of the second holes in the twins, adding a seed bead between each. Secure the beads with a turn-around stitch **(figure 3)**. Thread color is important since it will show between the beads.

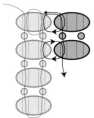

Figure 2

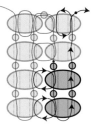

Figure 3

Right-Angle Weave

Right-angle weave (RAW) forms a flexible, open fabric of beads which can be added to on any side. Like ladder stitch, it can be done with one needle or two. Using two produces more even tension.

One Needle

Pick up four twins. Sew through the first three again to make a circle. Sew through the second hole of the bead the thread is leaving. Pick up three more beads. Sew through the starting bead again plus two more. Sew through the second hole of the bead the thread is leaving. Repeat. To move up to the next row, sew through all four beads again **(figure 1)**. The thread loop joining the four beads will always circle in the same direction.

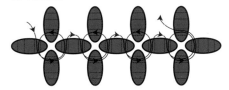

Figure 1

Row 2: Sew through the second hole of the bead that the thread is leaving. Pick up three twins. Sew through all four again, then the second hole of the bead that the thread is leaving. Pick up two beads. Sew through the nearest twin in the row below, plus three more. Repeat to the end of the row **(figure 2)**. The thread loop joining the four beads will always circle in the same direction.

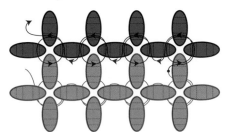

Figure 2

Two Needles

Attach a needle to each end of a length of beading thread. Pick up four twins and sew through the first one again. Tighten the ring of beads and center it on the thread. Cross the threads through the second hole. With one needle, pick up two beads. With the other needle, pick up one bead and sew through the last twin picked up with the first needle so that the threads cross. Cross the threads through the second hole. Repeat till the chain is one ring short of the desired length. Pick up three beads with the first needle **(figure 3, purple)**. Sew through the third bead with the second needle **(figure 3, green)**. Cross the threads through the second hole.

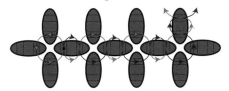

Figure 3

Row 2: Pick up three beads with the first needle **(figure 4, purple)**. Sew through the third bead with the second needle **(figure 4, green)**. Cross the threads through the second hole. With the first needle, pick up two beads **(figure 4, purple)**. With the second needle, sew through the second hole of the nearest twin in the row below, plus the last bead picked up **(figure 4, green)**. Repeat to the end of the row.

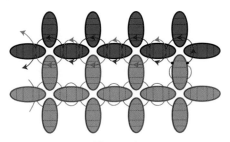

Figure 4

Wheat Stitch

Wheat stitch can be done only with twins. The shape of the twin closely resembles a grain of wheat and the two holes allow the beads to sit together in the same way that grains of wheat sit on the stem.

Row 1: Cut a length of thread and attach a needle to each end. With one needle, pick up one twin and three 15° seed beads. Sew through the second hole of the twin **(figure 1, purple)**. Repeat with the other needle **(figure 1, green)**. Center the beads on the thread.

Row 2: With one needle, pick up two twins and three seed beads. Sew through the second hole of the twin **(figure 1, purple)**. With the other needle, sew through the two twins just picked up. Pick up three seed beads. Sew through the second hole of the twin **(figure 1, green)**. Repeat row 2 as needed **(figure 2)**. To make the wheat tip, pick up one twin and three seed beads with one needle. Sew through the second hole of the twin **(figure 3, purple)**. With the other needle, sew through the twin. Pick up three seed beads. Sew through the second hole of the twin just picked up. Either end the threads at this point, or add another three seed bead embellishment on top of the twin, crossing the threads through the three beads and the last hole of the twin. If you prefer to use 11° seed beads, pick up two on either side of the twin.

Figure 1

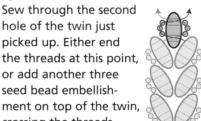

Figure 2

Figure 3

St. Petersburg Chain

As the name implies, St. Petersburg chain stitch originated in Russia. Rows are stitch up against each other but end up sitting diagonally. It can be done as a single or a double chain. Using twins works very well in this stitch because it saves a step.

Single Chain

Column 1: Pick up a contrast seed bead, two main color seed beads, two twins, and a contrast seed bead. Sew back through two twins and a main color bead.

Column 2: Pick up a contrast seed bead. Sew through the second hole of the two twins. Pick up two twins and a contrast seed bead. Follow the thread back through three twins. Repeat column 2 **(figure 1)**.

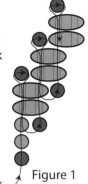

Figure 1

Double Chain

Cut twice the length of thread as for the single chain, and attach a stop bead at the center of the thread.

Column 1: Repeat column 1 of the single chain

Column 2: Pick up a decorative bead. Sew through the second hole of the two twins. Pick up two twins and one contrast. Follow the thread back through three twins. Repeat column 2 until you reach the desired length **(figure 2)**.

To begin the second half of the chain, undo the stop bead. Repeat column 1.

Column 2: Instead of picking up a new decorative bead, sew through the one that is already there. Stitch column 2 as you did for the first half. Repeat **(figure 3)**.

Figure 2

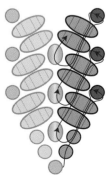

Figure 3

Netting

Circular

This type of netting looks much like a vintage crocheted doily. Modifications of this stitch are common and can produce intricate designs in shapes other than circles.

A tight circle of beads usually starts the netting, and the number of beads needed to complete each round becomes gradually greater. The twin provides the perfect joining bead between successive rounds of netting. In order to step up to the next round, the thread passes from the first hole to the second along the side of the twin. This means that the direction of the thread changes with each successive round **(figure 1)**.

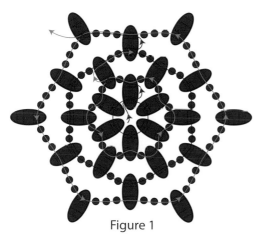

Figure 1

Flat

Netting made with twins appears to be more stretched out since the beads linking the two rows are longer. The thread passes from the first hole to the second along the side of the twin in order to turn around and begin the next row **(figure 2)**.

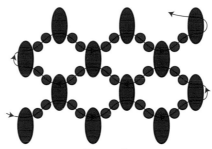

Figure 2

Tubular Stitches

All of the stitches explored so far are worked in a flat, two-dimensional shape. Many can be made tubular by joining a few stitches into a circle, moving up to the next round, and continuing on.

Tips

What if a bead breaks?
Beads are made of glass and can break if there is too much thread going through them or if the needle is too thick. If a bead breaks, you will need to undo your work to replace it.

What if the thread breaks?
You will need to undo your work until the thread is long enough to end or to join to a new piece.

Working with Thread

Moving from one hole to another when working with twins means that the thread passes along the bead. The thread may be visible as its direction changes. The change may not always be notated in the instructions.

Adding a Stop Bead

A stop bead is a temporary bead used to hold other beads in place. Sew through any seed bead that is a different color than the rest of the work. This will remind you to remove the stop bead, and avoids it accidentally becoming part of the design! Sew through the bead again. Be careful not to pierce the thread as you do this or the bead will be impossible to remove later.

Finishing the Thread

To end a thread, retrace any thread path through the work. Sew only where the thread has gone before, otherwise you may see the thread and the tension created may pull on the work in a strange way. Sew in about 2 in. (5cm) of thread in this manner, changing direction at least once. Along the way, tie several overhand knots (see Knots, p. 15). It is best to do this just before a large-hole bead so that the knot will move inside the hole when the thread is tensioned. Trim the thread close to the beadwork, taking care not to snip anything other than the tail. It may be useful to grasp the tail thread with a pair of pliers.

Adding More Thread

Working with more than 2 yd. (1.8m) of thread at once is not recommended. The thread becomes more easily snagged and knotted the longer it is. As you repeatedly pass the thread through the beads, it becomes worn and weakens. Some designs require a great deal of thread, so adding thread in the middle of a project is typical. There are a few methods of doing this:

1. Finish the thread at the point you are working, as if you were ending the project. Cut a new length of thread and sew it through the beads, following the thread paths and tying a few overhand knots along the way. Do not go through the same beads that were used to end the thread. Come out exactly where the first thread left off, and resume stitching.

Terms

"Sew through"
Sew through the designated bead, or beads, again in the same direction as the first time.

"Sew back through"
Sew through the designated bead, or beads, again in the opposite direction to the first time.

This method is good when the beads sit very closely together and getting a needle through them later would be difficult.

2. When 4–6 in. (10–15cm) of thread remains, cut a new piece. Tie the working thread to the new thread using a square knot (see Knots, below) 2–3 in. (5–7.6cm) from each end. Continue stitching, making sure that the loose end of the old thread stays in the work and the loose end of the new thread comes forward. Once you have gone a few beads past the knot, leave the ends to work in later. This method works best for intricate designs where the thread turns a good deal and the beads do not sit too closely together.

3. When 4–6 in. of thread remains, cut a new piece. Tie the working thread to the new thread using an overhand knot (see Knots, below), making sure that one loose end is just slightly longer than the other. Continue with stitching. The two loose ends will automatically be incorporated into the beadwork. This method works well for a continuous design, such as a rope, where it is unlikely that you will pass through beads again.

Knots
There are a few knots commonly used in beadwork. An overhand knot is usually done with a single thread end. Form a loop with the thread, and pass the end through the loop. It can also be made with two strands, to join them together.

A half-hitch knot is an overhand knot made over another thread between several beads.

A square knot is made with two thread ends, in two steps. Cross the right thread over the left, and then pass the right under the intersection. Cross the left thread over the right, and then pass the left under the intersection.

Opening and Closing Jump Rings
Jump rings are used in this book to attach beadwork to a finding. Grasp the jump ring with two pairs of pliers so that the opening is facing up between the two. Move one hand forward and the other backwards, opening the split in the ring. To close the ring, do the reverse. Never open a jump ring by pulling the two ends away from each other. The ring will never be round again or be able to close tightly. Open ear wires using the same method.

Bracelets

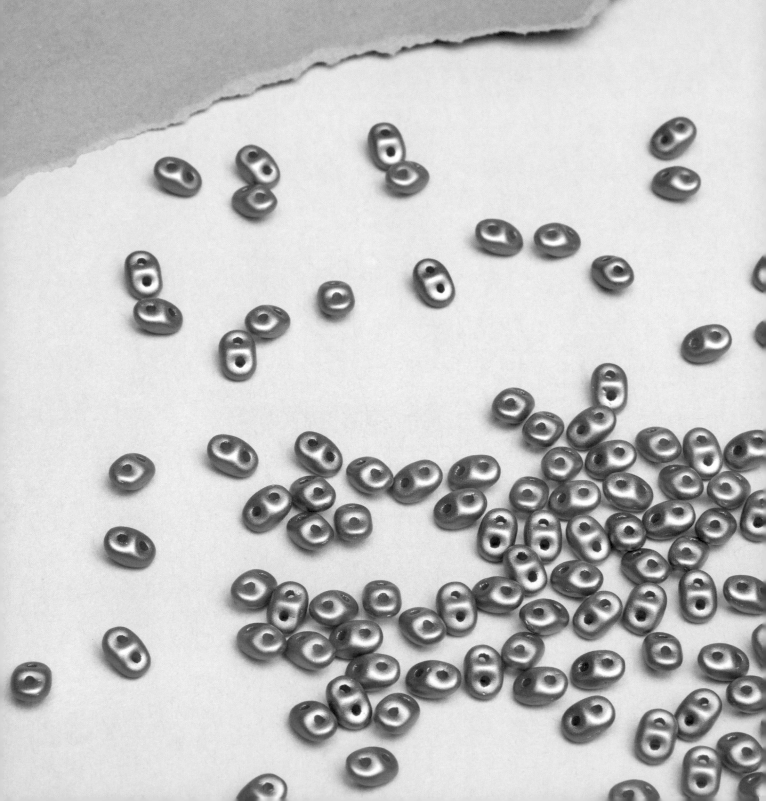

Duet Bracelet

Use familiar peyote stitch with two-hole beads to create a sturdy band of color. This easy bracelet is my tribute to the gift we can all enjoy: music! Music has been part of my life since I was a child taking piano lessons. This piece offers a great way to practice with these unique beads, and it's a beautiful gift for any musician in your life.

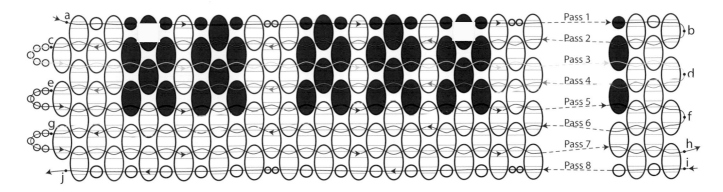

Figure 1

Materials

13g Czech twin or SuperDuo
  beads, color A (white luster)
6g twin or SuperDuos, color B
  (black opaque)
1g 11º Japanese seed beads,
  color C (white)
1g 11º Japanese seed beads,
  color D (black)
1g 15º rocailles, color E (white)
6 5mm 20-gauge jump rings,
  silver plated
21x6mm three-strand slide-lock
  clasp, silver-plated

Finished length
7 in. (18cm)

◯ Czech twin bead color A

⬤ Czech twin bead color B

◯ 11º seed bead

● 11º seed bead

o 15º rocaille

---

1. Cut 72 in. (1.8m) of thread. Attach
a needle to one end. Secure a stop
bead 8 in. (20cm) from the other end.

2. There are seven rows of beads but
eight passes of thread.
Pass 1: Pick up a color A twin bead, a
color C 11º seed bead, and an A. Pick
up As, color B twin beads, Cs, color D

11º seed beads, and color E 15º
rocailles in the following order: DBD,
A, DBD, AEEA, DBD, A, DBD, A, DBD,
AEEA. Repeat twice. Pick up DBD, A,
DBD. End with an A, a C, and an A
(figure 1, a–b). This makes three and a
half octaves of keys. The pattern is
symmetrical.

> **Don't work too tightly, or the
> bracelet will not curve nicely
> around your wrist.**

Pass 2: Sew through the second hole
of the last A added. Pick up an A.
Sew through the second hole of
the next A from the previous row.
Continue, using the following color
pattern: four Bs, an A, six Bs, and an
A. Repeat twice. End with four Bs and
two As **(b–c)**.
Pass 3: To make the first loop for the
clasp, pick up five Es and sew back
through the second hole of the last A
added. Loops for the other end will
be made between the seventh and
eighth rows. Pick up beads in the

following color pattern: two As,
BAB, two As, BABAB. Repeat
twice. End with two As, BAB, and
two As **(c–d)**.
Pass 4: Repeat pass 2 **(d–e)**.
Pass 5: To make the second loop for
the clasp, pick up five Es, and sew
back through the second hole of the
last A added. Peyote stitch 43 As into
the row **(e–f)**.
Pass 6: Peyote stitch 43 As into
the row **(f–g)**.
Pass 7: Repeat pass 5 to make the
third loop for the clasp **(g–h)**.

3. Make the loops for the clasp at
the other end of the bracelet: Pick
up an A and five Es. Sew through
the second hole of the A and then
through the A beside it. Change
direction and sew through the second
hole of the same bead **(figure 2, a–b)**.
Repeat twice **(b–c)**.

4. Zigzag through the last two beads
of each pass to exit at the last bead
of pass 7 **(c–d)**. Don't sew through the
A added for the clasp loop.
Pass 8: Sew through the second hole
of the last A added for pass 7. Pick up
a C, and sew through the second hole
of the next A. Repeat four times. Add
two Es between the next two As, then
six single Cs, two Es, and five single Cs.
Repeat twice to the end of the row
(figure 1, i–j).

5. To finish, follow the thread paths
back through the beads, tying three
or four overhand knots along the way.
Trim the thread. Undo the stop bead,
and repeat for the tail end. Attach the
clasp using jump rings.

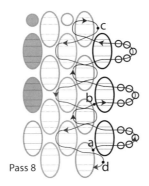

Pass 8

Figure 2

City Lights Bracelet

Working in square stitch is relatively easy with seed beads, particularly if they have a cylindrical shape. When a bead has two holes and it is shaped like a grain of rice, the stitch becomes a little more challenging—particularly if you are trying to put the narrow ends together. This bracelet was a nice way to feature a vintage black glass button; use something similar from your own stash.

Materials

17g Czech SuperDuo or twin beads
(silver Picasso)
12 4mm crystal bicones
(black or jet)
35 11º seed beads (Toho black)
6g 15º rocailles (Ceylon light gray)
22mm button with shank (black)

Finished length
7 in. (18cm)

 Czech twin bead

4mm crystal bicone

 11º seed bead

 15º rocaille

1. Cut a long but comfortable length of thread. Attach a needle to one end and a stop bead 16 in. (40cm) from the other end. Reserve the tail end for making the decreases at the button end of the bracelet.

2. Make a row of square stitch using seven SuperDuos with 15º seed beads in between (Techniques, p. 10). Add three 15ºs at the ends of each row when turning around **(figure 1, a–b)**.

3. Pick up a 15º, and stitch a second row. Add a 15º between the two SuperDuos at the end of the row **(d)**. Add three 15ºs at the ends of each row when turning around **(b–c)**.

4. For the third row, pick up a 15º and a SuperDuo. Sew through the second hole of the first SuperDuo picked up in row 2. Sew through the 15º and the first hole of the SuperDuo again **(figure 2, a–b)**. Pick up a bicone crystal and a SuperDuo, skip a Super-Duo from the previous row, and sew up through the next SuperDuo. Sew through the first hole of the SuperDuo again **(b–c)**. Resume regular square stitch, adding end-of-row embellishments. Sew through the crystal without adding any 15ºs **(c–d)**.

To add thread, finish the thread in the row that is being stitched. Add more thread by following the thread paths in the previous rows and exiting where the old thread left off. The beads sit closely together, and it's difficult to finish off threads once you have stitched past the loose ends.

5. Start the fourth row in the same way as the second and third, adding a 15º and a SuperDuo to the work. To get past the crystal, pick up a 15º and a SuperDuo twice. Sew through the SuperDuo in row 3 and then back through the first hole of the Super-

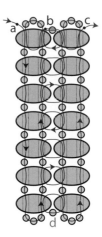

Figure 1

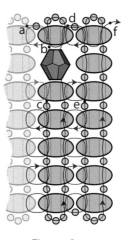

Figure 2

Duo just picked up **(d–e)**. Finish the row as before **(e–f)**.

6. These steps form the basic structure of the bracelet. Add a crystal to every second row, changing the location of the crystal up and down the row by one SuperDuo. Work a total of 25 rows.

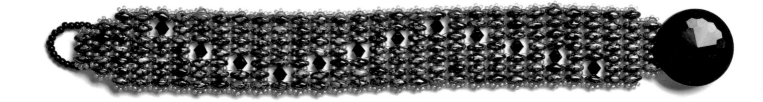

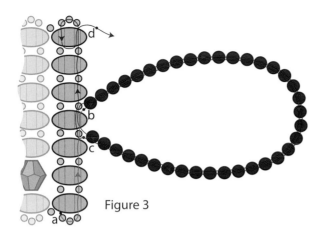

Figure 3

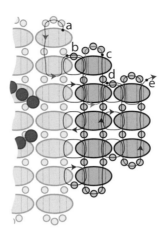

Figure 4

7. Add the loop for the button in the 26th row (no matter what size the button is, the bracelet will sit properly when worn): Add SuperDuos to the row as usual. To turn around, pick up three 15ºs, and sew through the second hole of the last SuperDuo added. Pick up a 15º, and sew through the second hole of the next SuperDuo. Repeat twice **(figure 3, a–b)**. Pick up 35 11º seed beads. Sew back through the SuperDuo.

Pick up a 15º, and sew and through all 35 beads again **(b–c)**. (Check the fit of the loop if your button is bigger than 22mm.) Sew through the 15º in front of the SuperDuo to which the loop is attached. Sew through the SuperDuo and the next 15º and Super-Duo. Finish the row as before **(c–d)**.

8. Stitch one more row of seven SuperDuos.

Option

To lengthen the bracelet, add an even number of rows to the overall pattern (divided between each end).

9. Row 28 uses five SuperDuos. Sew through the three 15ºs at the top of the row and down through the first SuperDuo, 15º, and second SuperDuo in the row. Sew under the bead and back up through the second hole of the SuperDuo **(figure 4, a–b)**. Stitch a row with five SuperDuos **(b–c)**. Prepare the 29th row by repeating a–b **(c–d)**.

Stitch a row with three SuperDuos. End with the thread leaving the first SuperDuo added in this row **(d–e)**. To finish, follow the thread path through the beads, tying several overhand knots along the way. Trim the thread.

10. Add a button to the other end of the bracelet: Undo the stop bead, turn the work around, and stitch two more rows, one with five SuperDuos and the other with three SuperDuos, repeating step 9 on the other end of the bracelet.

You might not find a vintage glass button exactly like mine, so use any button that is roughly the same size.

11. Make one more three-bead row to attach the button. Add the button in the same way as adding a crystal, stitching the shank where the crystal would go **(figure 5)**. Sew through the SuperDuos and button several times to strengthen the connection. To end, follow the thread path back through the beads, tying several overhand knots along the way. Trim the thread.

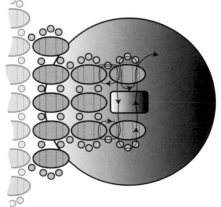

Figure 5

Nine-Patch Bracelet

Using right-angle weave (RAW) with twin beads produces a wonderful net-like fabric that has much potential as a base for beaded designs. This is just one example of how the stitch can be used. The pattern reminds me of the traditional nine-patch quilting block.

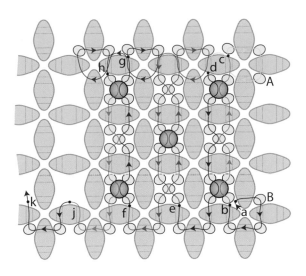

Figure 1

Materials

15g SuperDuos (antique turquoise)
47 2.5mm round smooth beads
    (gold-plated brass)
12g 11º Czech seed beads
    (pearl cream)
6 5mm 20-gauge jump rings
    (gold-plated)
21x6mm triple-strand slide-lock
    clasp (gold-plated)

Finished length
7¼ in. (18.5cm)

    SuperDuo

    11º seed bead

    2.5mm round bead

Bracelet

1. Cut 60 in. (1.5m) of thread. Use one of the two techniques for twin right-angle weave (Techniques, p. 11) to make a base that has 28 vertical columns of five SuperDuos each (the work should be ⅝ in./1.5cm shorter than the desired finished length). Add thread as needed. To finish, tie the two thread ends together into a square knot inside one of the small squares formed by the beads. With each end, follow the thread paths through the work, tying several overhand knots along the way. Trim.

Twin beads can work for this project, but the look would not be as uniform.

Add Embellishments

2. Cut a long length of thread. Attach a needle to one end and a stop bead 6 in. (15cm) from the other. Starting on the right-hand end of the base, sew through the SuperDuo in the lower right corner of the first full square, heading toward the edge **(figure 1, point a)**. Pick up an 11º seed bead, and sew through the nearest SuperDuo. Repeat twice (the thread path forms a loop) **(a–b)**.

   Pick up an 11º, a 2.5mm round, and an 11º. Sew through the SuperDuo at the opposite end of the square. Pick up three 11ºs. Sew through the SuperDuo at the opposite end of the square. Pick up an 11º, a round, and an 11º. Sew through the Super-Duo at the opposite end of the square **(b–c)**.

   Add an 11º between each of the three SuperDuos in the corner. Sew under the last 11º added inside the square, up through the first hole, and down through the second hole of the

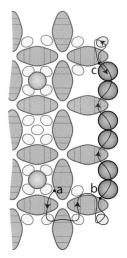

Figure 2

Option

To make the bracelet shorter, make one less nine-patch block and work enough plain RAW for the size needed. To make the bracelet longer, add rows of plain RAW.

horizontal SuperDuo at the edge **(c–d)**. Pick up an 11º, sew through the round already there, pick up an 11º, and sew through the second hole of the SuperDuo at the opposite end of the square. Pick up an 11º, sew through the middle of the three 11ºs already there, pick up an 11º, and sew through the second hole of the Super-Duo at the opposite end of the square. Pick up an 11º, sew through the round already there, pick up an 11º, and sew through the second hole of the SuperDuo at the opposite end of the square. Pick up an 11º, sew through the protruding SuperDuo at the edge, pick up an 11º, and sew through the closest hole of the next SuperDuo, into the next row of squares **(d–e)**.

3. Repeat b–e, adding a round to the middle square **(e–f)**. Repeat b–c **(f–g)**. Add an 11º between each of the two SuperDuos along the edge, working toward the right. Follow the thread path, sewing under the last 11º added inside the square, and down through the second hole of the horizontal SuperDuo at the edge. Follow the

thread path, sewing through the two SuperDuos and heading toward the edge. Add an 11º between each of the two SuperDuos along the edge. Sew down through the second hole of the horizontal SuperDuo at the edge **(g–h)**.

Repeat d–e **(h–j)**. Sew down into the second hole of the SuperDuo. Add an 11º between each of the two SuperDuos along the edge **(j–k)**. This completes one nine-patch embellishment.

4. Repeat steps 2 and 3 six more times, omitting the beads marked **A** and **B**. On the sixth repeat, add the beads marked **A** and **B** in the corresponding locations at the opposite end of the bracelet. End at the place corresponding to the start. Remove the needle. Don't cut the thread.

5. Undo the stop bead at the start of the work. Attach a needle to the tail end of the thread. Follow the thread path and sew through a SuperDuo, an 11º, a SuperDuo, an 11º, and a SuperDuo. Sew down through the second hole of the SuperDuo that the thread is leaving. Pick up an 11º, and sew back through the same hole

(figure 2, a–b). Pick up two rounds and sew through the SuperDuo at the edge of the RAW base. Repeat two more times. Pick up an 11º and sew back through the same hole **(b–c)**.

Follow the thread path back through the row of rounds, to the point where this step began. End the thread by following any thread path through the beadwork, tying several overhand knots along the way. Trim.

6. Repeat step 5 at the other end of the bracelet.

7. To attach the clasp, open all three 5mm jump rings. Slip a jump ring under the bridge made by two rounds along the edge of the bracelet and the other in the corresponding loop of one half of the clasp. Attach the remaining two loops of the clasp to the bracelet in the same way. Repeat for the other side.

Snowberry Bracelet

A piece made in St. Petersburg chain uses two rows of beads next to each other and requires a loop of thread to hold the two together. Using twin beads to make the stitch reduces a step. This easy design is a good introduction to working with twin beads.

Czech twin bead

 4mm round bead

 3mm fringe bead

 11º seed bead

• 15º cylinder bead

Materials

4g Czech twin or SuperDuo beads
    (opaque green pearl terra)
54 4mm crystal pearls (cream)
29 3mm fringe drop (gunmetal
    dark green)
2 11º seed beads (matte olive
    green
3g 15º cylinder beads
    (matte olive green)
10mm toggle clasp, silver

Finished length
6¾ in. (17.5cm) without clasp

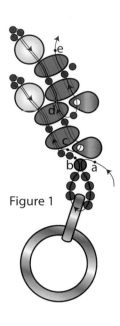

Figure 1

Bracelet

1. Cut 80 in. (2m) of thread, and attach a needle to one end. Pick up an 11º seed bead and seven 15º seed beads. Sew through the loop end of the clasp and the 11º again **(figure 1, a–b)**. Center the loop of beads on the thread. Wind half of the thread onto a bobbin or card and work with the other half.

2. Pick up two 15ºs, a twin bead, a 15º, a twin, a 4mm pearl, and three 15ºs. Sew back through the pearl, twin, 15º, and twin **(b–c)**. Pick up a 3mm drop. Sew through the second hole of the first twin. Pick up a 15º, and sew through the second hole of the second twin **(c–d)**.

3. Pick up a twin, a 15º, a twin, a pearl, and three 15ºs. Sew back through the pearl, twin, 15º, and twin just picked up, plus the next twin. Pick up a 15º and a drop. Sew through the second hole of the first twin. Pick up a 15º, and sew through the second hole of the second twin **(figure 1, d–e)**.

4. Repeat step 3 until the work has 13 pearls, or it is half the overall length needed, minus the length of the clasp. Don't cut the thread.

5. Undo the thread on the bobbin, and attach a needle to the end. Pick up two 15ºs, a twin, a 15º, a twin, a pearl, and three 15ºs. Sew back through the pearl, twin, 15º, and twin **(figure 2, a–b)**. Instead of picking up a drop, sew through the drop that was picked up in step 3. Sew through the second hole of the first twin. Pick up a 15º, and sew through the second hole of the second twin **(b–c)**. The drops will sit on top of the work. Make sure they all face the same way.

6. Pick up a twin, a 15º, a twin, a pearl, and three 15ºs. Sew back through the pearl, twin, 15º, and twin just picked up, plus the next twin. Pick up a 15º. Sew through the drop that was picked up in step 4 and the second hole of the first twin. Pick up a 15º, and sew through the second hole of the second twin **(c–d)**.

7. Repeat step 6 until the work is the same length as the first half. Don't cut the thread. Set aside.

8. Repeat steps 1–7 for the second half of the bracelet, using the toggle end of the clasp.

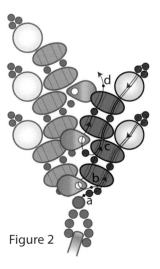

Figure 2

Join the Halves

9. Attach the needle onto the thread end that was used first. Pick up a twin, a 15º, a twin, a 15º, a pearl, and three 15ºs. Sew back through the pearl, 15º, twin, 15º, and twin **(figure 3, a–b)**. Pick up a 15º and a drop. Sew through the second holes of the two twins just added. Pick up a drop. Sew back through the second holes of the twins **(b–c)**. Remove the needle.

10. Attach the needle to the other thread end. Repeat step 9 using the drops already in place **(figure 4)**.

11. Go back to the other half of the bracelet. Repeat step 9. Instead of picking up a new pearl and three 15ºs, sew through the ones already there. Repeat step 10. Use the drops already there, as well as the pearl and three 15ºs **(figure 5)**.

12. Before finishing the threads, make sure each one is snug. Follow the thread paths back through the work, tying several overhand knots along the way. Trim the thread.

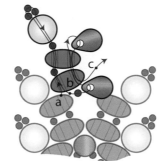

Figure 3

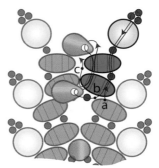

Figure 4

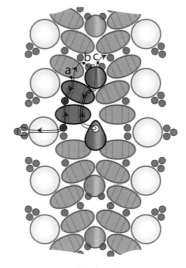

Figure 5

Option

Substitute 10º cylinder beads for fringe drops, and use red crystal pearls for a festive look.

Warp Speed Bracelet

When I started working with twin beads, my husband suggested that I try making a new stitch—something that couldn't work with single-hole beads. After some experimenting, this was the result. The long shape of the twin beads lends itself well to laying the beads in a basket-weave pattern.

Materials

Czech twin or SuperDuo beads:
  8g color A (silky copper)
  3g color B (silk dusty pink matte)
4g 15º rocailles (fancy rose pink)
2 5mm 20-gauge jump rings
  (copper)
18x13mm toggle clasp, copper

Finished length
7 in. (18cm)

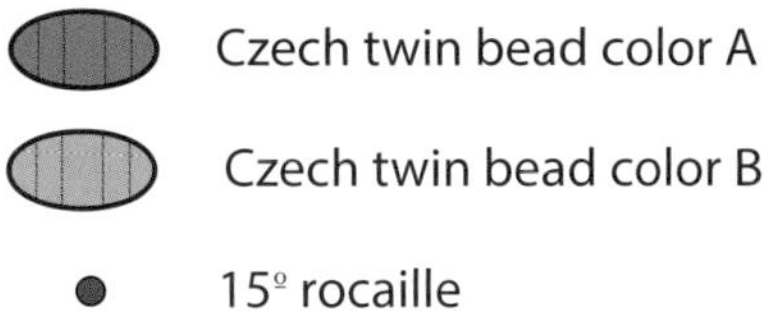

⬬ Czech twin bead color A

⬬ Czech twin bead color B

● 15º rocaille

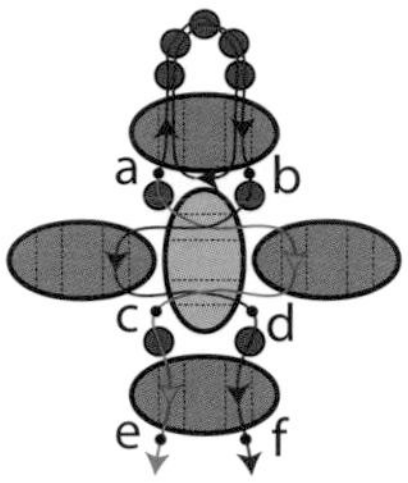

Figure 1

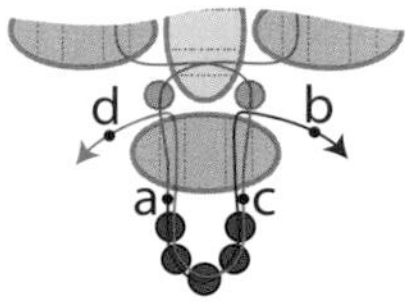

Figure 2

1. Cut 3 yd. (2.7m) of thread, and attach a needle to each end. Pick up a color A twin bead and five 15º rocailles. Sew through the second hole of the A. Follow the thread path again to make a loop **(figure 1, a–b)**, and center this loop on the thread.

Instructions are given for a two-tone bracelet. For a bracelet in only one shade, use twins of the same color.

2. With one needle, pick up a 15º, a color B twin bead, and an A. Sew through the second hole of the B **(figure 1, a–c)**. With the other needle, pick up a 15º, and sew through the first hole of the B. Pick up an A and sew through the second hole of the B **(b–d)**. With one needle, pick up a 15º

and an A **(c–e)**. With the second needle, pick up a 15º, and sew through the other hole of the A **(d–f)**. All of the As should be laying the same way and the B should be at right angles to the As.

3. Repeat step 3 until the work is the overall length needed, minus the length of the clasp. It is better to be slightly longer than shorter.

4. To make a loop for the clasp, use one needle to pick up five 15ºs. Sew through the second hole of the last A added **(figure 2, a–b)**. With the second needle, follow the thread path back through the 15ºs and into the other hole of the A **(c–d)**.

5. Remove the needle from one end of the thread. Wind this thread onto a bobbin or piece of card to use later.

6. Follow the thread path back through the next 15º, B, and A **(figure 3, a–b)**.

7. Pick up a 15º, a B, and an A. Sew through the second hole of the B. Pick up a 15º. Sew through the next wing-like A (through the hole that was already used) **(b–c)**. Repeat this step to the end of the row until the thread is exiting the last A.

8. Turn around by picking up three 15ºs and sewing through the second hole of the A that the thread is exiting **(figure 4, a–b)**.

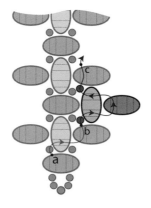

Figure 3

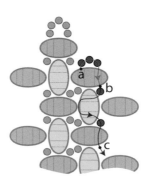

Figure 4

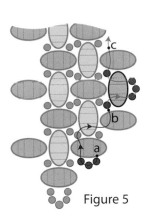

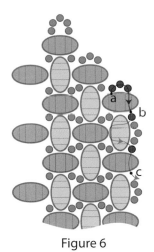

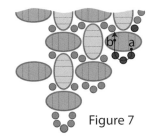

Figure 5   Figure 6   Figure 7

9. Pick up a 15º. Sew through the nearest hole of the B and its second hole. Pick up a 15º. Sew through the second hole of the nearest A **(b–c)**. Repeat this step to the end of the row until the thread is exiting the last A.

10. Turn around by picking up three 15ºs and sewing through the second hole of the A that the thread is exiting. Repeat step 6 **(figure 5, a–b)**.

11. Repeat step 7, replacing any A with three 15ºs **(b–c)**. Repeat this step to the end of the row until the thread is exiting the last A.

12. Repeat step 8 **(figure 6 a–b)**.

13. Repeat step 9 **(b–c)**. Repeat this step to the end of the row until the thread is exiting the last A.

14. Pick up three 15ºs, and sew through the second hole of the A that the thread is exiting **(figure 7, a–b)**. To end, follow the thread path back through the beads, tying several overhand knots along the way. Trim the thread.

15. Undo the thread reserved on the card. Turn the work around, and repeat steps 6–14 for the other half of the bracelet.

16. Use two pairs of pliers to open a jump ring. Insert one end into the loop of five 15ºs at the end of the bracelet and one half of the clasp. Close the jump ring. Repeat with the second half of the clasp at the other end of the bracelet.

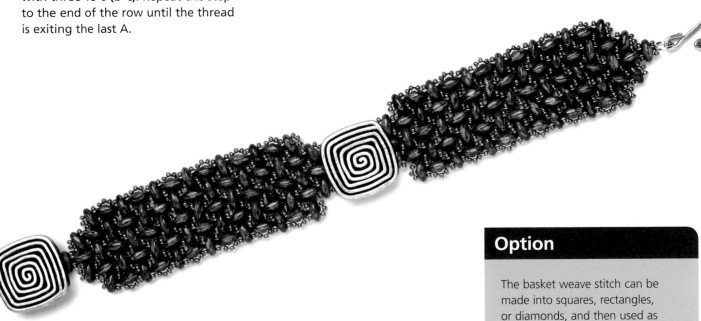

Option

The basket weave stitch can be made into squares, rectangles, or diamonds, and then used as components in jewelry designs.

Liberty Bracelet

Peanut beads and twin beads work very nicely together. Where one gets rounder, the other gets thinner. Where adjacent twins leave a space, the peanuts fill the space. Together the beads create these lovely medallions reminiscent of ice crystals.

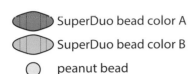

SuperDuo bead color A

SuperDuo bead color B

◯ peanut bead

● 15º seed bead

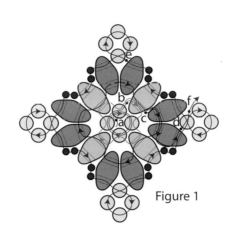

Figure 1

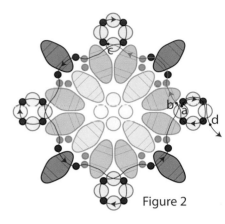

Figure 2

Materials

SuperDuo beads
  7g color A (chalk bronze
  lumi matte)
  2g color B (chalk picasso matte)
5g 2x4mm Japanese peanut beads
  (ceylon ivory)
2g 15º rocailles (transparent
  silver-lined bronze)
14mm toggle clasp (copper)

Finished length
7½ in. (19cm)

1. Cut 48 in. (1.2m) of beading thread and attach a needle to one end.
Round 1: Pick up four peanut beads. Sew through all four again. Leaving a 12-in. (30cm) tail, tie the working and tail ends into a square knot to make a tight circle of beads. Sew through the first peanut again **(figure 1, a–b)**.

> **This project is best made with SuperDuos. You can use twins if you cull any unevenly-shaped beads. Even SuperDuos have occasional defects. If you come across any, save them for the last round of the medallion, since only one hole is needed for those beads.**

Round 2: Pick up a color B SuperDuo and sew through the next peanut. Repeat three more times. Sew through the first B again **(b–c)**.
Round 3: Pick up two color A Super-Duos and sew through the same hole of the next B. Repeat three more times. Sew through the first two As again. Step up and change direction by sewing through the second hole of the last B **(c–d)**.

Round 4: Pick up four peanuts. Sew through the first peanut again and the second hole of the next A. Pick up two 15º rocailles, and sew through the next B. Pick up two 15ºs, and sew through the next A **(d–e)**. Repeat d–e three more times. End this round by sewing through the first peanut again **(e–f)**.
Round 5: Pick up a 15º, and sew through the next peanut in the small circle. Repeat three more times **(figure 2, a–b)**. Sew through the next A and 15º. Pick up a 15º, an A, and a 15º. Sew through the 15º of the round below that is closest to the A, as well as the A. Sew through the next peanut **(b–c)**. Repeat a–c three more times. Follow the thread path through the next peanut, 15º, peanut, 15º, and peanut **(c–d)**. You have completed the first square medallion. Don't end the thread.

2. In order to join the first medallion to the second using a continuous thread, you will work toward the center of the second by picking up a few beads from each round along the way. This means that the subsequent rounds will have some beads already

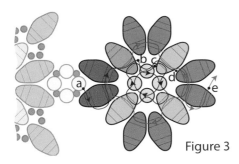

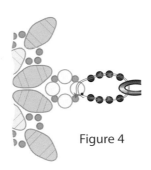

Figure 3

Figure 4

in place. To get to the center, pick up an A, and sew through the second hole. Pick up an A and a B **(figure 3, a–b)**.

Round 1: Pick up four peanuts. Sew through all of the peanuts again plus one more **(b–c)**. Pull up the beads into a tight ring.

Round 2: Pick up a B, and sew through the next peanut. Repeat twice. Sew through the B already there and the next peanut, making sure the motif is sitting properly. Sew through the first B again **(c–d)**.

Round 3: Pick up two As, and sew through the same hole of the next B. Repeat. Sew through the two As picked up at the start of this medallion and the next B. Pick up two As, and sew through the next B. Sew through the first two As again. Step up and change direction by sewing through the second hole of the last B **(d–e)**.

Rounds 4 and 5: These rounds are the same as the first medallion. Use the loop of peanuts from the first medallion in the second repeat.

Sometimes it is difficult to get the needle through two adjacent twins. Use a pair of pliers to gently pull the needle through if needed.

3. Make a total of eight medallions linked together. Add thread as needed. End with the thread exiting at **figure 2, point d**.

4. To attach the clasp, pick up four 15ºs, one end of the toggle, and four 15ºs. Sew through the peanut that the thread is leaving, all the beads and toggle, and the peanut again **(figure 4)**. Follow the thread path back through the work, tying several overhand knots along the way. Trim the thread.

5. Attach a needle to the tail end of the thread. Follow the thread paths through the work so the thread is exiting the same peanut as shown in **figure 2, point d**. Repeat step 4 to attach the other end of the toggle. Finish the thread off in the same way.

To make the bracelet shorter, make one less medallion and adjust the number of beads near the clasp to get a good fit. To make the bracelet longer, add beads to the loop near the clasp, or add an entire medallion.

Options

- Create a nice pendant with two or three medallions in a row, or even one by itself.
- Make two single medallions for a pair of cute earrings. Attach an earring wire to the SuperDuo in the corner for a different look. Make a few pairs in new color combinations.

Aleksandra Bracelet

Russian spiral stitch is a form of tubular peyote. Because you use an asymmetrical variety of beads to create this stitch, the design begins to spiral. Depending on what kinds of beads you choose, the effect can be quite stunning.

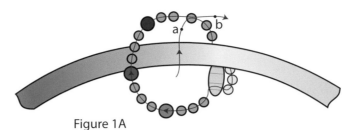

Figure 1A

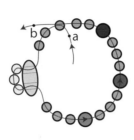

Figure 1B

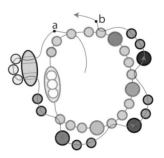

Figure 2

Materials

7g Czech twin or SuperDuo beads,
color A (crystal labrador)
11º Czech seed beads
    4g color B (periwinkle blue)
    4g color C (opaque navy AB)
    4g color D (silver lined cobalt)
15º rocailles
    5g color E (gold luster
    medium blue)
    10g color F (transparent silver-
    lined silver)
10 in. (25cm) 4mm synthetic rubber
    or plastic tubing
2 8–9mm bead caps (silver)
12mm magnetic clasp

Finished length
8¾ in. (22.5cm)

1. Cut 72 in. (1.8m) of thread. Attach a needle to one end and a stop bead 6 in. (15cm) from the other end. Pick up three color E 15º rocailles, a twin bead, and three color F 15º rocailles. Sew through the second hole of the twin. Pick up three Es, a color B 11º seed bead, three Es, a color C 11º seed bead, three Es, a color D 11º seed bead, and two Es. Sew through the first E, forming a ring of beads. Insert the length of rubber or plastic tubing into the circle of beads. It doesn't matter which way you stitch; the pattern works both clockwise and counter clockwise **(figures 1A and 1B, a–b).**

Laying the beads in small piles on my bead mat, in correct color order, helped me keep the pattern sequence correct.

2. Pick up a twin and three Fs. Sew through the second hole of the twin. Pick up two Es. Sew through the first E added after the twin in the first round. Pick up a B and two Es. Sew through the first E added after the B in the first round. Pick up a C and two Es. Sew through the first E added after the C added in the first round. Pick up a D and two Es. Sew through the first E added after the D the first round **(figure 2, a–b).**

Key:
- Czech twin bead color A
- 11º seed bead color B
- 11º seed bead color C
- 11º seed bead color D
- 15º seed bead color E
- 15º seed bead color F

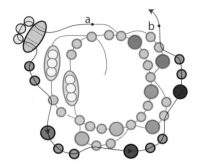

Figure 3

3. Repeat step 2 until you reach the desired length. Add thread as needed. End with a D. The third round is shown in **figure 3, a–b**. The twin beads will begin to sit upright, with the three Fs sitting on top, pointing outward. The first few rounds are a bit tricky. They can cross over each other. When the spiral reaches the desired length, trim the rubber or plastic tubing to sit just below the last twin.

4. There are three rounds under the bead cap. For the first round, substitute one B for the group of one twin and three Es. End the round at the new B, which will mean that five 11⁰s have been used **(photo a)**. For the second round, pick up a B, C, or D and only one E, four times **(photo b)**. For

the third round, sew through only the four Es. Sew through all the Es again for security.

5. Pick up the bead cap (wide end first), three Bs, three Es, one end of the magnetic clasp, and three Bs. Sew back through the bead cap and the third E of the last round. Do not tighten the thread **(photo c)**. Sew through the bead cap, beads and clasp again, and the first E of the last round. Tighten the thread. If possible, follow the thread path through the bead cap, beads, and clasp a third time. Retrace the thread path back through the spiral, tying several overhand knots along the way.

6. Repeat steps 4 and 5 on the other end of the work.

Option

When choosing a new color scheme for your bracelet, make each bead a different shade. The bracelet becomes far more interesting when the colors "rub" against each other a little.

Rings and Earrings

Europa Earrings

Bead netting is a versatile stitch that can be used to create many projects. Circular netting reminds me of vintage crocheted doilies. These earrings are two tiny doilies joined together, padded with a metal donut. They are easy to make, so you can have several pairs to coordinate with your wardrobe.

Materials

5g Czech twin or SuperDuo beads
  (opaque teal pearl terra dyed)
1g 11º Czech seed beads (opaque
  turquoise)
2g 15º rocailles (transparent
  silver-lined ice blue)
2 20–22mm metal donuts
pair of ear wires (silver or
  silver-plated)

Finished length
1¼ in. (3.2cm)

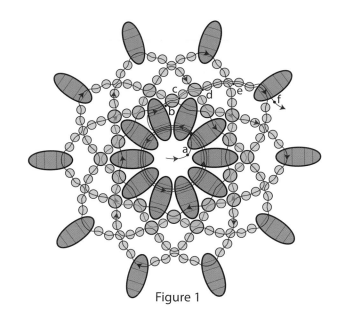

Figure 1

 Czech twin bead

⬭ 11º seed bead

○ 15º cylinder bead

1. Cut 24 in. (60cm) of thread and attach a needle to one end.
Round 1: Pick up 10 twin beads, and sew through all of the twins again, leaving a 4-in. (10cm) tail. Tie a square knot and sew through two more twins. Sew through the second hole of the twin that the thread is leaving **(figure 1, a–b).**

> It will be very difficult to end the tail thread in round 1. Use the needle to work the tail thread back through one or two twins. Step up to start the next round by going through the second hole of the twin that the tail is leaving.

Round 2: Pick up an 11º seed bead, and sew through the second hole of the next twin. Repeat nine more times. Step up to start the next round by sewing through the first 11º again **(b–c).**

Round 3: Pick up a 15º seed bead, an 11º, and a 15º. Sew through the next 11º of the round below. Repeat nine more times. Step up to start the next round by sewing through the first 15º and 11º again **(c–d).**
Round 4: Pick up five 15ºs and sew through the next 11º of the round below. Repeat nine more times. Step up to start the next round by sewing through the first three 15ºs again **(d–e).**
Round 5: Pick up two 15ºs, a twin, and two 15ºs. Sew through the third (middle) 15º of the row below. Repeat nine more times. Step up to start the next round by sewing through the first two 15ºs and the twin again **(e–f).**

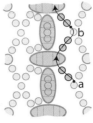

Figure 2

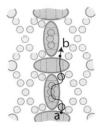

Figure 3
(side view)

Figure 4
(side view)

Round 6: Pick up a 15º, a twin, and five 15ºs. Sew through the second hole of the 15º, pick up a 15º, and sew through the next twin in the round below, using the hole that already has thread in it **(figure 2, a–b)**. This loop is larger than all the others and becomes the point of attachment for the ear wire. Pick up a 15º, a twin, and three 15ºs, sew through the second hole of the 15º, pick up a 15º, and sew through the next twin in the round below, using the hole that already has thread in it **(b–c)**. Repeat b–c eight more times **(c–d)**. End the thread by sewing through the bead-work along existing thread paths, tying several overhand knots along the way. Trim the thread. End the tail thread the same way. Set this half of the earring aside.

2. Make a second earring half by repeating rounds 1–4.

Round 5: Hold the completed half behind the current work. Pick up two 15ºs. Instead of picking up a new twin, sew through the unused hole of the nearest twin in round 5 of the completed half. Pick up two 15ºs. Sew through the third (middle) 15º of the

row below **(figure 3)**. Repeat four more times. Insert the donut in between the two halves. Resume stitching the round. Step up to start the next round by sewing through the first two 15ºs and the twin again.

Round 6: Pick up a 15º. Follow the thread path through the twin, three (or five) 15ºs, and the second hole of the twin added in round 6 of the first half. Pick up a 15º and sew through the next twin in the round below, using the same hole **(figure 4)**. Repeat nine more times. End the thread by sewing through the beadwork along existing thread paths, tying several overhand knots along the way. Trim the thread. End the tail thread the same way.

3. Open an ear wire with two pairs of pliers. Insert it into the five-bead loop on the edge of the pendant. Close the wire.

4. Make a second earring.

Dahlia Ring

In some of the twin beads that I bought, I noticed that a coating on one half of the bead made a beautiful color on the other half. But in order to view the color in its entirety, the holes in the bead needed to be face up. This posed a whole new design challenge, which I embraced in this ring.

Figure 1

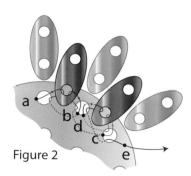

Figure 2

Figure 3

Materials

2g twin beads (crystal vitrail)
2g Japanese cylinder beads
   (silver-lined gold)
7x5mm teardrop-shaped pearl
11º seed bead, any color
2 13mm domed perforated disks,
   gold-plated

Finished size
Ring top is ⅞ in. (22mm) in
   diameter

 Czech twin bead

cylinder bead

 7x5mm teardrop pearl

1. Cut 36 in. (90cm) of thread. Attach a needle to one end and a stop bead 4 in. (10cm) from the other end. Hold one perforated disk with the domed side towards you. Sew through any second-row hole of the disk from the underside **(figure 1, a–b)**. Sew through a nearby edge-row hole of the disk, from the underside. Pick up a twin bead from the front. Sew through the same hole in the disk **(b–c)**. Pull the thread up snugly. Sew through the next edge-row hole of the disk, from the underside. Pick up a twin from the front of the bead. Sew through the same hole in the disk **(c–d)**. Repeat, working around the outside row of holes. End with the thread coming up through the first hole used.

2. The second round has twins sitting between the outer row of holes. Pick up a twin from the front. Sew through the same hole in the disk and then up through the second hole **(figure 2, a–b)**. Sew through the front of the twin just picked up, down through the second hole, and up through the third hole **(figure 2, b–c)**. Pick up an A from the front. Sew down through the same hole in the

disk and then up through the second hole **(figure 2, c–d)**. Sew through the front of the twin just picked up, down through the second hole, and up through the third hole **(figure 2, d–e)**. Repeat a–e around the row of holes. End the round by sewing through any second-row hole in the disk.

3. Add six twins between each of the six holes using the attachment stitch of step 2 **(figure 3)**. End the round by sewing through the center hole.

4. Pick up the teardrop pearl. Sew back through the center hole. Pick up an 11º seed bead and sew back through the hole, the pearl, and the hole **(figure 4)**.

5. Reinforce any stitches where needed. Undo the stop bead at the tail end of the thread. Tie the working thread and tail end together into a square knot. Sew under several of the thread bridges at the back of the work, tying overhand knots along the way. Trim the thread ¼ in. (6mm) away from the knot. Set aside.

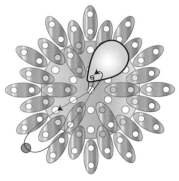

Figure 4

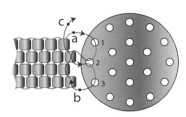

Figure 5

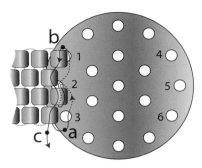

Figure 6

6. Cut 36 in. (90cm) of thread. Attach a needle to one end and a stop bead 6 in. (15cm) from the other end. Pick up four 11⁰s, and work a strip of regular even-count peyote stitch that is approximately 30 rows long. Undo the stop bead and attach the needle to the tail thread.

7. Pick up the second perforated disk with the domed side toward you. Hold it near the peyote strip so that three outer edge holes line up with the strip **(figure 5)**. Sew down through hole 1, up through hole 2, through the first "out" bead on the peyote strip, down through hole 2, and up through hole 3 **(figure 5, a–b)**. Follow the thread path through the four 11⁰s of the last peyote row **(figure 5, b–c)**.

8. Stitch the next row of peyote, adding two 11⁰s. Sew down through hole 3 and up through hole 2. Sew through the second 11⁰ just added and then under it down through hole 2. Sew up through hole 1 **(figure 6, a–b)**. Follow the thread path through the four 11⁰s of the peyote row just completed **(figure 6, b–c)**. End the tail thread by following the thread path through the peyote band, tying several overhand knots along the way. Trim the thread.

9. Reattach the needle to the working thread. Test the band for length. If it fits, repeat step 7, attaching the end of the peyote band to holes 4, 5, and 6 (refer to **figure 6**). Test the band

once more for fit. If the fit is not good, undo the work, and either add or remove 11⁰s from the peyote band. If the fit is good, repeat step 8 **(photo)**. Sew down through hole 5.

10. Place the beaded disk over the disk with the peyote band attached, so the outer rows of holes match. Stitch the two disks together by sewing through matching edge holes, then moving on to the next pair. Once you are all the way around, change direction and sew around again for added security. End the thread by

sewing through the same pair of holes five or six times and tying off with two overhand knots. Sew through several holes towards the opposite end of the disks and trim the thread.

The great thing about making a beaded ring is that it can be custom-fit to any size finger.

Options

- If you don't like the gold color of the perforated disk showing through the beads, coat the disk with nail polish in your preferred shade. This may require more than one application.
- The ring would also look great in any non-coated twin bead or SuperDuo color.

Khione Earrings

The little rose-colored chatons used in this pair of earrings are two-hole beads in their own right. They offer just the right amount of effervescent sparkle. Accent the chatons with a few more bicone crystals for even more shine.

Materials

14 Czech twin or SuperDuo beads
  (silky silver)
8 4mm crystal bicones (crystal AB)
2 6mm xilion chatons in silver-
  plated two-hole setting (rose)
8 11º Japanese cylinder beads
  (silver-lined crystal)
4 11º Japanese seed beads (black)
1g 15º rocailles (transparent
  silver-lined silver)
pair of lever-back ear wires
  (silver or silver-plated)

Finished length
1¾ in. (4.4cm)

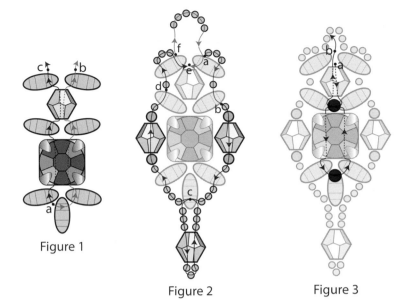

Figure 1

Figure 2

Figure 3

 Czech twin bead

 4mm crystal bicone

 6mm xilion chaton in
  two-hole setting

 11º cylinder bead

● 11º seed bead

○ 15º rocaille

1. Cut 16 in. (40cm) of thread and attach a needle to each end. With one needle, pick up two twin beads, a xilion chaton, a twin, a 4mm bicone crystal, and a twin **(figure 1, a–b)**. With the other needle, pick up a twin, sew through the second hole of the chaton, pick up a twin, sew through the crystal, and pick up a twin **(b–c)**. Center the beads on the thread.

2. Turn the work so that the chaton is facing up. With the right needle, pick up three 15º rocailles, and sew through the second hole of the twin that the thread is leaving. Pick up a 15º, and sew through the second hole of the twin below **(figure 2, a–b)**. Pick up a 15º, an 11º cylinder bead, a crystal, a cylinder, and a 15º, and sew through the second hole of the

nearest twin in the group of three twins under the chaton. Pick up three 15ºs, and sew through the next twin **(b–c)**. Pick up three 15ºs, a crystal, and three 15ºs, sew back through the crystal, pick up three 15ºs, and sew through the second hole of the last twin used **(c–c, red)**. Pick up three 15ºs, and sew through the second hole of the next twin. Pick up a 15º, a cylinder, a crystal, a cylinder, and a 15º, and sew through the second hole of the twin above the chaton **(c–d)**. Pick up a 15º, and sew through the second hole of the nearest twin. Pick up three 15ºs and sew through the hole the other thread is leaving **(d–e)**.

3. With the left needle, pick up six 15ºs. Sew through the twin at the point where the right needle began in step 2 **(f–e)**. This forms a loop in which to insert the ear wire. Making sure the work is snug, tie the two ends into a square knot.

4. Still using the left needle, sew through the crystal. Pick up an 11º seed bead, and sew through the left hole of the chaton, plus the twin underneath it. Pick up an 11º. Sew through the other twin under the chaton and the right hole of the chaton. Cross through the 15º picked up first, and sew through the crystal again **(figure 3, a–b)**.

5. Finish the thread by following the thread paths through the work, tying several overhand knots along the way. Repeat for the other thread end.

6. Open an ear wire using two pairs of pliers. Slip it into the loop of six 15ºs at the top of the earring, making sure it will be facing the right way. Close the ear wire.

7. Repeat steps 1–6 to make a second earring.

Options

Replace the chaton with a pair of back-to-back Tila beads, making the earrings reversible, or use a round bead in the center for a completely new look.

Prairie Spring Earrings

Two-hole beads form interesting structural beadwork components. In this design, one twin is used to support two others thereby creating a dual-layer start. I discovered that the best solution to making the base was a twin combined with a SuperDuo. I like the pastel shades, reminiscent of the prairie in spring.

Materials

30 or **40** SuperDuo beads (seafoam
   turquoise green)
14 or **18** Czech twin beads
   (orange dyed)
16 or **20** 4mm crystal pearls
   (rose peach)
14 or **18** 4mm crystal bicones
   (crystal AB)
2g 11º cylinder beads (transparent
   silver-lined silver)
pair of lever-back ear wires
   (silver-plated)

Finished length
1¼ in. (3.2cm)

⬭ SuperDuo bead

⬭ Czech twin bead

● 4mm glass pearl

⬙ 4mm crystal bicone

• 11º seed bead

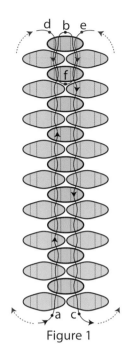

Figure 1

Follow the instructions for a pair of large earrings, starting with 18 Super-Duos and nine twin beads to create the first circle, or make a smaller version (as in the photo on p. 46) using 14 SuperDuos and seven twins.

1. Cut 40 in. (1m) of thread, and attach a needle to each end. Pick up a SuperDuo and a twin bead nine times **(figure 1, a–b)**. Leave a 4-in. (10cm) tail, and sew through the second hole of the last twin picked up. Pick up a SuperDuo, and sew through the second hole of the next twin. Repeat seven more times, ending by picking up a SuperDuo **(b–c)**. Lay the beads on your work surface. The working end of the thread should be at **point c**. Insert the needle into the beads at point e, and sew through three holes **(e–f)**. Insert the tail end needle into the beads at point d, and sew through three holes **(d–f)**. Tighten the threads to make a snug circle of beads.
   Tie a square knot at point f. With the working end of the thread, follow the thread path through several beads, ending with a SuperDuo, then

through the second hole of the SuperDuo. Finish the tail end of the thread. Follow the thread path through the alternating SuperDuos and twins, tying several overhand knots along the way. Trim the thread.

Finishing off the tail end now is much easier than waiting until you complete the motif.

2. Continue with the working thread. Pick up two 11º seed beads, a 4mm pearl, and two 11ºs. Sew through the unused hole of the next SuperDuo on the same side **(figure 2, a–b)**. Repeat eight more times. End by sewing through the first two 11ºs and the pearl picked up at the start of this round **(b–c)**.

3. Pick up two 11ºs, sew through the next SuperDuo on the opposite side to the previous round, pick up two 11ºs, and sew through the next pearl **(figure 3, a–b)**. Repeat eight times. End by sewing through the first two 11ºs added and the next SuerDuo **(b–c)**.

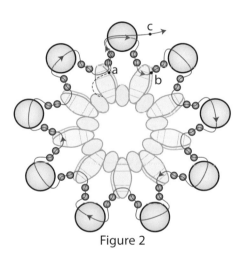

Figure 2

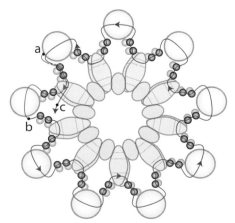

Figure 3

The little beads between the pearl and the green SuperDuos sometimes get pushed behind the pearl. Use a needle or small hook to nudge them into place.

4. Pick up three 11ºs. Sew through the next SuperDuo **(figure 4, a–b)**. Repeat eight times **(b–c)**. Sew through a pair of 11ºs from the previous round, a pearl, and then two 11ºs and a SuperDuo on the opposite side. Repeat a–c on that side. End by sewing through a pair of 11ºs and a pearl **(c–d)**.

Figure 4 shows this step from one side only.

5. Pick up a 4mm bicone crystal, and sew through the next pearl. Repeat seven more times **(d–e)**. Pick up a crystal, three 11ºs, a SuperDuo, two 11ºs, a pearl, two 11ºs, a SuperDuo, and six 11ºs **(e–f)**. Sew through the second hole of the last SuperDuo picked up, pick up two 11ºs, sew back through the pearl, pick up two 11ºs, sew through the second hole of the first SuperDuo picked up, and pick up three 11ºs. Sew through the first crystal picked up, in the same direction as the first time, plus the next pearl along the outer edge of the circle **(f–g)**. End by following the thread path along the outer round of the circle at least once (or as far as the thread will allow), tying several overhand knots along the way to secure. Trim with a sharp scissors.

6. Open an ear wire with two pairs of pliers. Insert it into the loop of six 11ºs at the top of the earring. Close the wire. Make a second earring.

Figure 4

Options

- Connect large circular motifs for a lovely necklace.

48

Erica Earrings

Even though twin beads have two holes, it's not always necessary to use both. When I made some beaded beads using only one of the holes, they ended up looking like miniature sea urchins. I discovered that one of my editor's favorite colors is navy blue, so I've named the earrings after her.

Materials

60 Czech twin beads (opaque teal pearl terra dyed)
2 7–8mm beads, any material in blue, black, or any color
2 4mm round beads (opaque navy)
2g 11º Czech seed beads (opaque navy)
pair of 2-in. (5cm) kidney-shaped ear wires (silver)
2 1½-in. (3.8cm) headpins (silver)
permanent marker or nail polish (dark blue or black)

Extra tools
sewing pin or needle
roundnose pliers
wire cutters

Finished length
2⅝ in. (6.8cm)

 Czech twin bead

 11º seed bead

1. If the 7–8mm beads you have chosen are not blue or black, color them with a permanent marker or nail polish. Lay out 30 twin beads in six piles of five beads each on your work surface.

2. Cut 16 in. (40cm) of thread and attach a needle to one end.
Round 1: Pick up five 11º seed beads. Sew through all five 11ºs again to form a snug ring. Leaving a 3-in. (7.6cm) tail, tie the two ends into a square knot. Sew through the first 11º again **(figure 1, a–b)**.
Round 2: Pick up a twin, and sew through the next 11º on the ring. Repeat four times, using all the twins from one pile on your work surface.

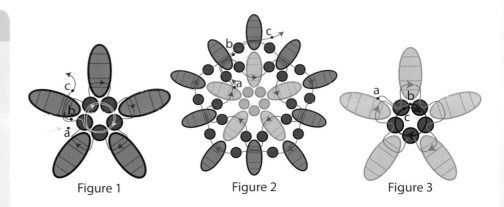

Figure 1   Figure 2   Figure 3

Step up to the next round by sewing through the first twin again **(b–c)**.
Round 3: Pick up an 11º, a twin, and an 11º. Sew through the next twin of the previous round, using the same hole that the thread passed through in that round. Repeat four more times, using all of the twins in the next pile. Step up to the next round by sewing through the first 11º and twin again **(figure 2, a–b)**.
Round 4: Repeat round 3 **(b–c)**.
Rounds 5–7: Repeat round 3 three more times. As the work grows, it can become difficult to see when the round is finished and when you need to step up to the next row, so rely on the small piles of beads set up at the start. At the end of round 7, slip a 7–8mm round bead into the netting formed. It may be useful to insert a sewing pin or needle into the first round of 11ºs and through the inner bead so you don't lose the location of the hole.
Round 8: Pick up an 11º, and sew through the next twin of the previous round, using the same hole. Repeat four times. Step up to the next round by sewing through the first 11º again **(figure 3, a–b)**.
Round 9: Sew through all five 11ºs of the previous round two times **(b–c)**. Tie an overhand knot in this round. End by following the thread path

through the work, tying several overhand knots along the way. Trim.

3. Attach a needle to the tail thread. End by following the thread path through the work, tying several overhand knots along the way. Trim.

4. Make a second beaded bead.

5. Assemble an earring by stringing an 11º, a beaded bead, and a 4mm round bead on a headpin. Make a simple loop above the 4mm using a pair of roundnose pliers. Insert an ear wire into the loop. Repeat this step to assemble the second earring.

Option

If you have twin beads left over from other projects, make a collection of these miniature beaded beads. String them between other beads for a fun and colorful necklace.

De Vine Earrings

In my initial experimentation with twin beads, I found I could make them sit diagonally, one on top of the other, by putting some seed beads underneath. The curve formed looked like the serrated edge of a leaf. Combine a few leaves to make a cute pair of earrings. I made these earrings with both purple and copper twins to go with the necklace in the Gallery on p. 108, but you can choose matching colors, if you like.

Ropes

Gilana Necklace

This quick project is a great option for fast-and-easy beading. The necklace can be made to any length and in any color scheme.

Materials

8g Czech twin beads (transparent crystal bronze-lined)
40 8mm glass pearls (brown or bronze)
4g 11º Czech seed beads (transparent bronze)
6g 15º Charlottes (metallic gold)
11x7mm lobster claw clasp (gold plated)
2 18-gauge 5mm jump rings (gold plated)

Finished length
22 in. (56cm)

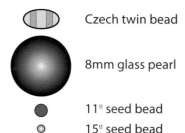

Czech twin bead

8mm glass pearl

11º seed bead

15º seed bead

The necklace uses one length of thread in three passes.
1. Cut 10 ft. (3m) of thread, and attach a needle to one end. To start the first pass, pick up an 11º seed bead, a twin bead, and three 15º seed beads, sew through the second hole of the twin, pick up an 11º, an 8mm pearl, an 11º, a twin, and three 15ºs, and sew through the second hole of the twin. Pick up an 11º **(figure 1, a–b)**, and center the beads on the thread. Wind one half of the thread onto a bobbin or card to use later.

2. Pick up a pearl, an 11º, a twin, and three 15ºs, sew through the second hole of the twin, and pick up an 11º **(b–c)**.

3. Repeat step 2 until you have used 20 pearls, or the work is half the desired length.

4. Unwind the thread from the bobbin, and attach a needle to the end. Repeat steps 2 and 3 using the other half of the thread.

5. Make a turn-around loop for the end of the rope: Pick up seven 15ºs, sew through all seven 15ºs again, and then sew back through the last 11º added **(figure 2, a–b)**. Repeat at the other end of the work.

6. Stitch the second pass: Pick up a twin and three 15ºs, and sew through the second hole of the twin plus the next 11º, pearl, and 11º from the first pass **(c–d)**.

7. Repeat step 6 until you reach the other end of the rope and the thread is exiting the last 11º.

8. Stitch the third pass: Attach the needle onto the long remaining thread. Pick up a twin and three 15ºs. Sew through the second hole of the twin. Sew through the next 11º, pearl, and 11º from the first pass, making sure that the twin sits neatly against the other two beneath it **(figure 3)**. The twins form a three-pointed star shape as shown in the **photo**. Repeat until you reach the other end of the rope and the thread exits the last 11º.

Options

Try this design with round or faceted gemstone or crystal beads.

9. Sew through the 15ºs of the loop and back through the last 11º. To end, follow the thread path back through the beads, tying several overhand knots along the way. Trim the thread. Repeat this step with the other end.

10. To attach the lobster claw clasp, open a jump ring with two pliers. Insert the jump ring into a bead loop at the end of the rope and into the loop on the clasp. Close the jump ring. Attach the second jump ring to the loop at the other end of the rope.

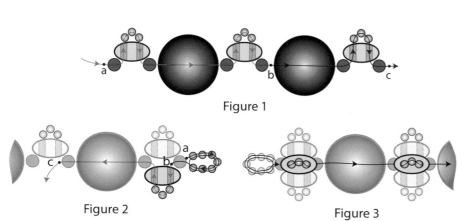

Figure 1

Figure 2

Figure 3

Mossy River Necklace

Leaving the second hole of the twin beads unused in this project creates a unique raised texture on the surface of the necklace. I really like the way this rope supports itself and how slinky it feels. This project is very easy to make.

Czech twin bead

● 11º seed bead color A

● 11º seed bead color B

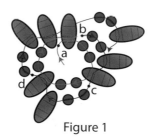

Figure 1

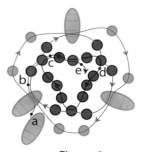

Figure 2

Materials

55g Czech twin beads (opaque green iris)

11º Czech seed beads
  25g color A (transparent dark green)
  6 color B (black)

2 10x5mm bead caps (gold)

2 18-gauge 6mm jump rings (gold-plated)

32x21mm gold toggle clasp, or other large clasp

Extra tools

chopstick or round, narrow knitting needle

Finished length

25¼ in. (63cm)

Make sure you have enough supplies to complete the project. Each 4 in. (10cm) of rope uses approximately 150 twin beads (8–9g), and 39 in. (100cm) of thread stitches about 3½ in. (9cm) of rope.

Necklace

1. Cut a very long, but comfortable, length of thread. Attach a needle to one end and a stop bead 10 in. (25cm) from the other. Pick up a twin bead, and then two color A Czech seed beads and a twin three times. Sew through the first twin picked up, using the same hole **(figure 1, a–b)**. Insert a chopstick or dowel into the circle of beads. Pick up two As and a twin, sew through the next twin picked up **(b–c)**, pick up two As and a twin, and sew through the next twin picked up **(c-d)**. Take care that the last beads added sit on the correct side of the work already done. It does not matter if you work from left to right, right to left, clockwise or counter-clockwise. Repeat c–d until the rope

measures the desired length, adding thread when needed. Work around a chopstick or dowel until the rope is long enough to hold in your hand.

Ensure that there is at least 10 in. (25cm) of thread left when the rope is the desired length. If not, undo a few rounds, add some thread, and re-stitch the rounds.

2. The last round worked is shown in **figure 2, a–b**. To end, pick up three As and sew through the next twin. Repeat two more times. Sew through the first two As added **(b–c)**. Pick up an A, a color B 11º seed bead, and an A, and sew through the middle A of the next three As in the previous round **(c–d)**. Repeat twice. Sew through the first A and B added in this round **(d–e)**.

3. Pick up the wide end of a bead cap and seven As. Sew back through the beadcap and the next B. Repeat twice, using a different B each time. Tighten the threads. Sew back through the beadwork, following the previous thread paths. Tie several overhand knots along the way. Trim the thread.

4. Undo the stop bead at the beginning of the rope. Attach a needle to the tail end thread. Repeat steps 2 and 3.

5. Open a jump ring. Insert it into the seven-bead loop at one end of the rope and a ring on the loop end of the toggle clasp. Close the jump ring. Repeat with the second jump ring at the other end of the rope, using the bar of the toggle clasp.

Options

- This silver-and-red rope looks very different than the green one, even though its also made with tubular peyote. Stitch through the second hole of the Twin bead rather than using the same hole twice. The rope is not self-supporting, so you will need to insert 4mm synthetic rubber or plastic tubing.
- Wear these ropes with the toggle at the front.

Viking's Double Necklace

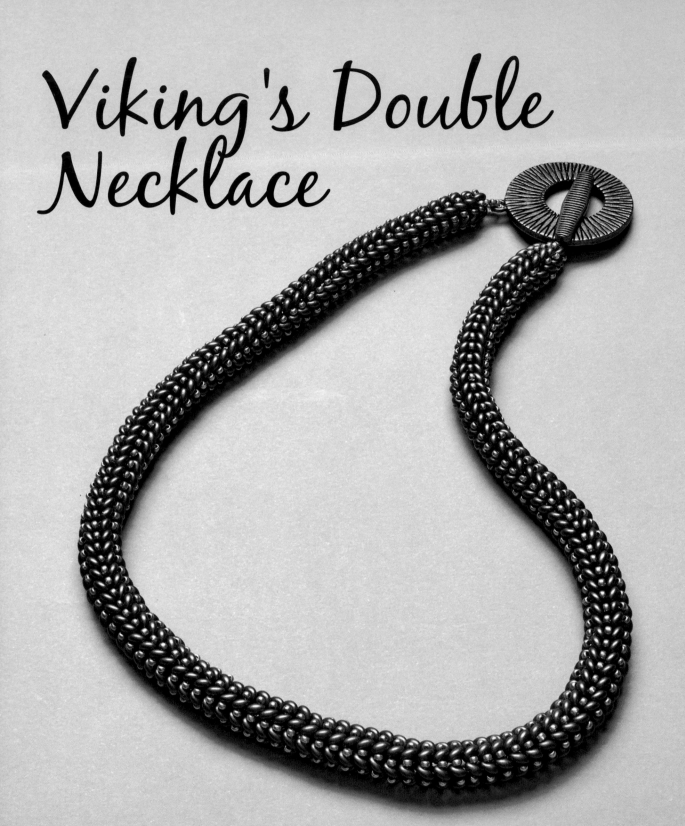

This rope reminds me of a Viking knit chain I made using copper wire. It's named the Viking's Double because it uses twin beads, it copies the wire version, and it is twice as thick!

Materials

45g Czech twin or SuperDuo beads
   (metallic copper)
9g 11º Czech seed beads
   (galvanized metallic copper)
38mm copper toggle clasp

Extra tools
skewer or knitting needle

Finished length
21 in. (53cm), excluding clasp

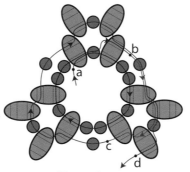

Figure 1

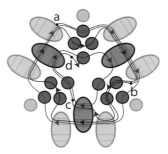

Figure 2

 Czech twin bead

 11º seed bead

Sewing through the second hole of a twin bead usually means that the thread changes direction. However, in this rope the thread does not change direction with each round, which keeps the tension more even.

1. Cut a long but comfortable length of thread. Add a needle to one end and a stop bead 9 in. (20cm) from the other end.

2. Pick up a twin bead, an 11º seed bead, a twin, and two 11ºs. Repeat twice. Sew through all of the beads again to form a ring, plus the first twin and 11º. Make sure that the needle does not pierce the thread as you sew around the ring a second time. This round is a holding row and will have to be undone at the end. Step up to the next round by sewing through the second hole of the next twin in the ring without changing the direction of the thread **(figure 1, a–b)**.

3. Pick up an 11º, sew through the second hole of the next twin in the ring, pick up a twin, an 11º, and a twin, and sew through the second

hole of the next twin in the ring **(b–c)**. Repeat twice. Follow the thread path through the first 11º again, the next two twins, and the next 11º. Step up to the next round by sewing through the second hole of the next twin in the ring without changing the direction of the thread **(c–d)**. The diagram shows the thread loose. Once it is tightened, it will form a ring. Work around a skewer or knitting needle, if desired.

4. Repeat step 3 until the work is the desired length (my rope has 137 rounds). Add more thread as needed.

5. To end, pick up an 11º, and sew through the second hole of the next twin in the ring. Pick up a twin, and sew through the second hole of the next twin in the ring. Repeat twice. Follow the thread path through the first 11º added in this round and the next three twins **(figure 2, a–b)**.

6. Pick up two 11ºs, and follow the thread path through the next three twins. Repeat twice. Sew through the next two 11ºs and a twin, and step up to the next round by sewing through the second hole of the next twin in the ring **(b–c)**.

7. Pick up an 11º, and sew through the next twin. Repeat twice. Sew through all of the beads again, exiting a twin **(c–d)**.

8. Attach the loop end of the toggle closure first: Pick up three 11ºs, the small loop on the clasp, and three more 11ºs. Skip two beads in the last round of the rope, and sew through the next 11º. Sew back through the 11ºs just picked up, the clasp, and the remaining 11ºs. Sew through the first twin again in the same direction as the first time. Follow the thread path of this step once more to strengthen the work. Then follow the thread path back through the beads in the main rope, tying several overhand knots along the way. Trim the thread.

9. To finish the other end of the rope, undo the stop bead and the first round of work until you have removed eight 11ºs. The thread should be exiting a twin. Turn the work around and attach a needle to the thread. Pick up a twin, an 11º, and a twin. Sew through the second hole of the next twin in the ring. Repeat twice. Follow the thread path through the 11º that was already there, the next two twins, and the next 11º. Step up to the next round by sewing through the second hole of the next twin in the ring.

10. Repeat steps 5–7. Repeat step 8 to add the toggle end of the clasp, picking up 12 11ºs, the small loop on the toggle, and and 12 11ºs. Finish off in the same manner as the other half of the clasp.

Theodora Necklace

This rope necklace incorporates twin beads into tubular herringbone stitch like an embroidery sampler would use various cross-stitches to make an alphabet. Add more colors, or expand your favorite section to create a whole new look.

Materials

15g Czech twin beads (metallic copper mix)

6g Tila beads (dark bronze opaque metallic)

10g 11º Japanese seed beads (gold galvanized frost)

10x6mm magnetic clasp (bronze or copper)

Finished length
21¾ in. (55cm)

 Czech twin bead

 Tila bead

 11º seed bead

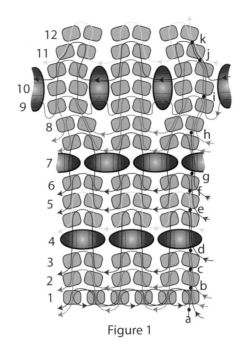

Figure 1

---

1. Cut a long length of thread. Attach a needle to one end and a stop bead 6 in. (15cm) from the other end. Start ladder stitch by picking up two 11º seed beads. Sew through the 11ºs again so that the two beads are sitting against each other with their holes parallel. Pick up an 11º, and sew through the previous again as well as the new one. Repeat until six 11ºs have been used. Join the first bead to the last to form a ring (figure 1, a–b).

> The rope necklace is made up of two patterned sections that alternate—a 2-in. (5cm) smooth area and a 1-in. (2.5cm) section resembling a pinecone. Note that the illustrations show the work as if it were flat. The thread path shown includes the step-up to the next round.

2. Begin with the smooth section of rope (the ring of beads is round 1). Work rounds as follows:

Round 2: Pick up two 11ºs, and sew down through the 11º below on the ladder and up through the next 11º. Repeat twice to the end of the round, sewing up through the first bead again (b–c). This is one round of tubular herringbone stitch.

Round 3: Repeat round 2 (c–d).

Round 4: Pick up a twin bead and two 11ºs. Sew down through the second hole of the twin, the 11º below in the previous round, and up through the next 11º. Repeat twice, and step up to the next round by sewing through the twin and the first 11º (d–e).

Rounds 5 and 6: Work two rounds of tubular herringbone, sewing through only the 11ºs of round 4 in round 5 (e–f, f–g).

Round 7: Pick up a twin, two 11ºs, and a twin. Sew down through the 11º below in the previous round, up through the next 11º, and through the second hole of the second twin picked up. Pick up two 11ºs and a twin. Sew down through the 11º below in the previous round, up through the next 11º, and through the second hole of the third twin picked up. Pick up two 11º. Sew down through the unused hole of the first twin picked up, through the 11º

below in the previous round, up through the next 11º, and through the first hole of the first twin picked up. Step up to the next round by sewing through the 11º above the hole in the twin just sewn through (g–h).

Rounds 8 and 9: Work two rounds of tubular herringbone, sewing through only the 11ºs of round 7 in round 8 (h–i).

Round 10: Pick up four 11ºs. Sew down through the next 11º in the round below. Pick up a twin. Sew up through the next 11º in the round below. Repeat twice. Step up to the next round by sewing through the first two 11ºs picked up (i–j).

Round 11: Pick up two 11ºs, and sew down through the third 11º picked up in the row below, the second hole of the twin, and up through the second of four 11ºs picked up in the row below. Repeat twice (j–k). Step up to the next round by sewing through an 11º.

Rounds 12–18: Repeat rounds 8, 7, 6, 5, 4, 3, and 2, in that order. This completes the smooth section.

63

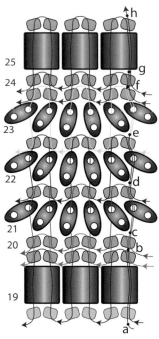

Figure 2

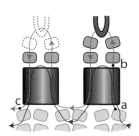

Figure 3

3. Work the pinecone section as follows:

Round 19: Pick up a Tila bead and two 11ºs. Sew down through the second hole of the Tila, down through the 11º in the row below, and up through the next 11º. Repeat twice. Step up to the next row by sewing through the Tila and first 11º picked up **(figure 2, a–b)**.

The two faces of a Tila bead are not exactly the same, so pick them up in the same orientation when using them in this design.

Round 20: Work a round of tubular herringbone, sewing through only the 11ºs of round 19 **(b–c)**.

Round 21: Pick up a twin, two 11ºs, and a twin. Sew down through the 11º in the row below and up through the next 11º. Repeat twice. Step up to the next row by sewing through the first twin and 11º picked up **(c–d)**. Make sure that the unused holes of the twins face outward **(photo)**.

Rounds 22 and 23: Repeat round 21 twice, sewing through only the 11ºs of the previous round **(d–e, e–f)**.

Round 24: Repeat round 20 **(f–g)**.

Round 25: Repeat round 19 **(g–h)** to complete the pinecone section.

4. Make a total of eight smooth sections alternating with seven pinecone sections, adding thread as needed.

5. Attach the clasp: Pick up a Tila, and sew down through the second hole. Skipping an 11º in the previous round, sew down into the next 11º and up through the 11º beside it. Repeat. Sew up through the first Tila

(figure 3, a–b). Pick up two 11ºs, sew through half of the clasp, pick up two 11ºs, and sew down into the second hole of the Tila. Sew up into the next Tila, pick up an 11º, sew through the second 11º, clasp, and third 11º above the other Tila, pick up an 11º, and sew down into the second hole of the Tila **(b–c)**. Repeat b–c for added strength. End by following any thread path back through the work, tying several overhand knots along the way. Trim the thread.

6. Undo the stop bead at the beginning of the rope. Repeat step 5 to attach the other half of the clasp.

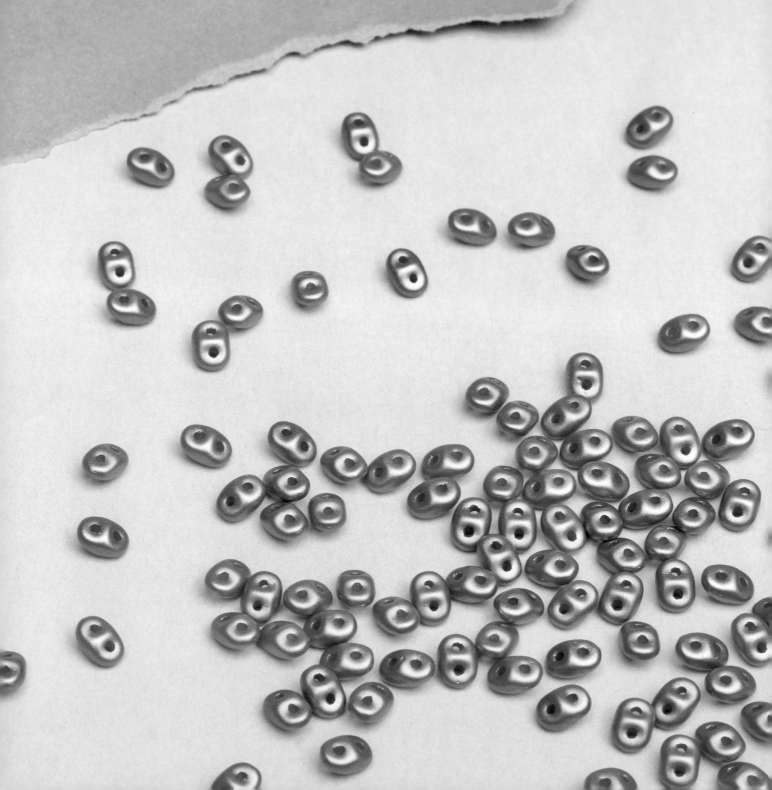

Chains and
Pendants

Delft Lace Necklace

Designs don't always have to be complicated to be beautiful. Here, two-hole Tilas meet two-hole twins in a lacy necklace that can display your favorite Bali bead, pendant, or charm.

Materials

18mm Bali silver bead, lampworked
   bead, charm, or pendant
7g Czech twin or SuperDuo beads
   (opaque gunmetal)
30 Tila beads (opaque matte
   cobalt)
3g 11º (Czech beads, hematite)
3g 15º Japanese seed beads
   (matte royal blue)
2 18-gauge 5mm jump rings
   (silver-plated)
10–12mm lobster claw clasp
   (silver-plated)

Finished length
23½ in. (60cm)

twin bead

Tila bead

11º seed bead

15º seed bead

Figure 1

Figure 2

1. Cut 96 in. (2.4m) of thread. Attach a needle to each end. (One needle will be called the pink needle and the other green. They will correspond to the pink and green thread paths in the illustrations.)

2. With the pink needle, pick up three 15º seed beads and a Tila bead; with the green needle, pick up two 15ºs. Sew through the second hole of the Tila **(figure 1, a–b)**, and center the beads on the thread.

3. With the pink needle, pick up a 15º, an 11º seed bead, a twin bead, and three 15ºs. Sew through the second hole of the twin. Pick up a 15º and an 11º. With the green needle, pick up a 15º, and cross the pink thread through the first 11º. Pick up a twin, and three 15ºs. Sew through the second hole of the twin. Pick up a 15º, and cross the pink thread through the 11º **(b–c)**. With the pink needle, pick up a 15º, a twin, and three 15ºs. Sew through the second hole of the twin. Pick up an 11º. With the green needle, pick up a 15º, a twin, and three 15ºs. Sew through the second hole of the twin, and cross the pink thread through the 11º **(c–d)**. With the pink needle, pick up a 15º and a Tila. With the green needle, pick up a 15º, and sew through the second hole of the Tila **(d–e)**.

4. Repeat step 3, b–e, 14 times.

5. With the pink needle, pick up a 15º, an 11º, a twin, and three 15ºs. Sew through the second hole of the twin. Pick up a 15º and an 11º. With the green needle, pick up a 15º. Cross the pink thread through the first 11º. Pick up a twin, and sew through the second hole. Pick up a 15º, and cross the pink thread through the second 11º **(figure 2, a–b)**. With the pink needle, pick up two 15ºs and an 11º. With the green needle, pick up a 15º, a twin, and three 15ºs, then sew through the second hole of the twin. Repeat. Pick up a 15º, and cross the pink thread through the 11º **(b–c)**. With the pink needle, pick up a 15º, a twin, and three 15ºs. Sew through the second hole of the twin. Pick up an 11º, a 15º, and a Tila. With the green needle, pick up a 15º. Sew through both holes of the first twin picked up by the green thread, crossing its own path. Cross the pink thread through the 11º.

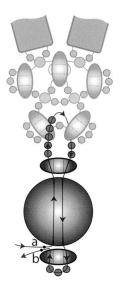

Figure 3

Pick up a 15°, and sew through the second hole of the Tila (c–d).

6. Continue the chain by repeating step 3, b–e, until it is as long as the other side.

7. Pick up five 15°s with one needle, and sew through the opposite hole in the Tila. With the second needle, trace the thread path through the 15°s but in the opposite direction. With one needle, sew through the next 15° and 11° in the chain. With the other needle sew only through a 15°. Tie the two ends into a secure square knot. With each needle, follow the thread paths in opposite directions back through the work, tying several

overhand knots along the way. Trim each thread.

8. Cut 12 in. (30cm) of beading thread. Attach a needle to one end and a stop bead 3 in. (10cm) from the other. Pick up the chosen focal bead (from the bottom), a twin, and seven 15°s. Pass the needle through the space between the lowest twins at the turning point of the chain, and sew through the second hole of the twin just picked up and the focal bead again. Pick up a twin and three 15°s. Sew through the second hole of the twin (**figure 3, a–b**). Snug up the loop of beads. Follow the thread path back through all of them again. Tie a square knot where points a and b meet. End by following the thread paths again to hide the tails. Trim.

9. Open a jump ring. Insert it into the loop of 15°s at one end of the necklace and the ring on the lobster clasp. Close the ring. Open the second jump ring, and insert it into the loop of 15°s at the other end of the necklace.

Options

Make a shorter length and use it for a bracelet. Add eyeglass holder findings and make a fabulous chain to keep track of your reading glasses.

Twin Helix Necklace

Fig

12. Wit
two thr
path of
directio

13. Usir
again, p
Lay the
face-up
made. S
the dro
of the f
of the c
11° of t
Pick up
second
large dr
path ba
tying se
the way

14. Usin
follow t
but in th
the thre

15. Atta
using or
threads:
and five
second h
thread l
the othe
originate

When twin beads are strung with small beads in between they look like rungs on a ladder. I used this pattern frequently and have named it vertical ladder stitch. I wondered if I could somehow make it spiral, much like a strand of DNA. It took a good deal of trial and error to make it work, but eventually I did! My dad was the one who taught me not to give up—it must be in the family DNA.

Marrakesh Necklace

Lef

This

1. C
atta
need
six 1
11º
(figu
the

2. Pi
twin
Sew
15º,

3. Pi
11º,
path
previ
just p
seed
befo

4. Re

5. Tu
need
twins

A structure that fascinates me is a beaded bead. I have experimented with this particular design before—twelve pentagons put together to make something round. Using twin beads provided a whole new way of making the sphere. It needed something to hang from, and the matching spiral rope, itself a logical structure, is the perfect answer.

Beaded Bead Pendant

The beaded bead is made from two rows of five pentagons each, topped by a pentagon as the "lid" and another as the bottom. In this case, an obvious pentagon shape is made of five twin beads stitched together in a ring. Smaller beads fill in the spaces and form a triangle. The pentagon of five twins looks like a person. For ease of instruction, the uppermost twin will be called the head, the next two will be left and right arms, and the lower two will be left and right legs. Even if the pentagon is standing on its head, the same terms will be used **(figure 1)**.

> **The direction of the thread changes frequently but this does not matter. The most important thing is to be working on the correct "leg."**

1. If the 19mm bead is not a suitable color, paint it with a layer of nail polish. Let dry thoroughly.

2. Cut 40 in. (1m) of beading thread and attach a needle to one end. Leaving a 6-in. (15cm) tail, pick up five twins. Sew through all five again, plus the first one, to make a tight ring. This is upside-down pentagon 1 (refer to figure 1). Sew through the second hole of the A the thread is leaving, changing direction **(figure 2, a–b)**. Sew a bit of colored thread into the second hole of pentagon 1's left leg, to use as a point of reference.

3. Pick up a color B 11º seed bead, a color A 11º seed bead, a B, a twin, a B, an A, and a B. Sew through the twin again to make a snug ring **(b–c)**. Pick up a B. Sew through the twin just picked up, back through the B, and through the twin again **(c–d)**. Follow the thread path through the B, A, B, and twin, then through the second hole of the twin **(d–e)**. The last twin picked up forms the left leg of right-side-up pentagon 2 (refer to figure 1).

4. Pick up four twins. Sew through five twins and the four just picked up so that the thread is exiting the right leg of pentagon 2. Sew through the second hole of this twin, changing direction **(figure 3, a–b)**.

5. Repeat step 3, b–e **(b–e)**. The last twin picked up forms the left leg of upside-down pentagon 3 (refer to figure 1).

6. Pick up four twins. Sew through five twins and the four just picked up so that the thread is exiting the left arm of pentagon 3. Sew through the second hole of this twin, changing direction **(figure 4, a–b)**.

7. Pick up a B, an A, and a B. Sew through the right arm of pentagon 1. Pick up a B and an A. Sew through the two As below the legs of pentagon 2 and back through the A **(f)**. Pick up a B. Sew through the left arm twin of pentagon 2 **(b–c)**. Pick up a B. Sew through the right arm twin of pentagon 1, back through the B, and through the twin again **(c–d)**. Sew through the other hole of the twin and follow the thread path through the ring of twins until the thread exits the right arm of pentagon 3. Sew through the second hole of this twin **(d–e)**. The three pentagons will sit together in a slight bowl shape.

Materials

19mm bead, any material
3 14x8mm faceted briolettes, pressed glass or crystal (black)
8x6mm rondelle, pressed glass or crystal (black)
19g Czech twin or SuperDuo beads (iris brown)
11º Czech seed beads
   6g color A (iris brown)
   10g color B (red)
19x12mm toggle clasp (antique gold)
2 6mm 20-gauge jump rings (copper)
nail polish to match beads
colored thread scrap

Finished length
Rope 20½ in. (52cm)
Pendant 2¼ in. (6cm)

- Czech twin bead
- 11º seed bead color A
- 11º seed bead color B

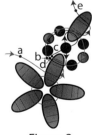
Figure 2

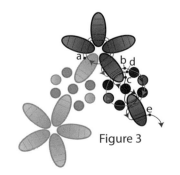
Figure 1

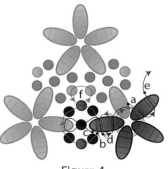
Figure 3

Figure 4

Figure 5

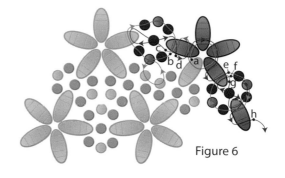

Figure 6

8. Repeat step 3, b–e **(figure 5, a–d)**. The last twin picked up forms the left leg of right-side-up pentagon 4 (refer to figure 1).

9. Pick up four twins. Sew through five twins plus one more. Sew through the second hole of this twin, changing direction **(figure 6, a–b)**.

10. Pick up a B and an A. Sew through the two As above the legs of pentagon 3 and back through the A. Pick up a B. Sew through the right arm of pentagon 2. Pick up a B, an A, and a B. Sew through the left arm of pentagon 3 **(b–c)**. Pick up a B. Sew through the right arm of pentagon 2, back through the B, and through the twin again **(c–d)**. Sew through the other hole of the twin and follow the thread path through the ring of twins until the thread exits the right leg of pentagon 4. Sew through the second hole of this twin **(d–e)**.

11. Repeat step 3, b–e **(e–h)**.

12. Repeat steps 6–11 to make a total of 10 pentagons. Refer to figure 1 for the order of stitching the pentagons. Finish with the thread exiting the second hole of the right arm of pentagon 10.

13. Join the right arm of pentagon 10 with the left arm of pentagon 2 using As and Bs, as in previous steps. Next, join the right leg of pentagon 10 with the left leg of pentagon 1 **(photo a)**. Then join the left arm of pentagon 9 with the right arm of pentagon 1. End by exiting the second hole of the heads of any pentagon in the odd-numbered row.

14. Repeat steps 3 and 4.

15. Using this new pentagon as the "lid", attach each one of the twins to the heads of each pentagon in the row below using As and Bs, as in previous steps **(photo b shows one**

completed). The thread will always have to come to the center, move to the next twin, and then move into the second hole of that twin. End by following any thread paths through the beadwork to come out in the second hole of the heads of any pentagon in the even-numbered row **(photo b)**.

16. Sew a piece of colored thread through the 19mm bead to keep track of where the hole is. Insert it into the cup of beadwork made so far. Repeat step 15 with the bottom of the bead. To finish, follow any thread path through the work, tying several overhand knots along the way. Repeat with the tail thread. Line up the hole of the inner bead, using the colored thread, with opposing three-A triangles **(photo c)**.

Spiral Rope

17. Cut a long length of beading thread and attach a needle to one end. Pick up three twins, two Bs, an A, and two Bs. Sew through the three twins again **(figure 7, a–b)**. Pick up a twin, two Bs, an A, and two Bs. Sew through the last two twins added in the first loop plus the twin picked up in this loop **(b–c)**. Push the seed beads to the left. Repeat b–c until you have used 124 twins or the rope has reached the desired length. Add thread as needed. Set this half of the rope aside.

18. Make the second half of the rope by repeating step 17. Push the seed beads to the right each time so that the rope will spiral the other way **(figure 8)**. Work until 121 twins have

Figure 7

Figure 8

Figure 9

been used or the rope is three twins shorter than the first half.

19. Pick up a twin. Instead of picking up two Bs and an A, sew through two Bs and an A in the third-to-last group of seed beads at the end of the other rope **(photo d)**. Pick up two Bs and finish the stitch. Pick up a twin. Sew through two Bs and an A in the second-to-last group of seed beads at the end of the other rope. Pick up two Bs and finish the stitch **(photo e)**. Pick up a twin. Sew through two Bs and an A in the last group of seed beads at the other end of the rope. Pick up two Bs and finish the stitch.

20. Finish all four ends of the rope by following the thread path back through the beads, tying several overhand knots along the way. Trim the threads.

Attach the Beaded Bead Pendant

21. Cut 56 in. (1.4m) of beading thread and attach a needle to each end. Pick up a twin, 12 As, a briolette, and three As. Sew back through the briolette, all of the As, and the second hole of the twin. Center the beads on the thread **(figure 9, a–b)**. With one needle, sew down through the other hole of the twin. Pick up 10 As, a briolette, and three As. Sew back through the briolette, all the As, and the same hole of the twin. Pick up an A **(b–c)**. With the other needle, repeat b–c, picking up eight As **(a–d)**.

22. With one needle, sew through the beaded bead, pick up an A, the rondelle, and an A. With the other

needle, follow the thread path through the beaded bead, the A, and the rondelle. Sew through the last A so the threads cross.

23. Bring the ropes to your work area. Find the center two twins at the point where the two ropes join. The last A picked up will sit between them. With one needle, sew through the unused hole of the twin on the right. With the other needle, sew through the unused hole of the twin on the left **(photo f)**.

24. Put one needle and thread aside. With the other needle, pick up an A and sew through the unused hole of the next twin in the spiral. Repeat all the way along the rope. This will tighten the twist. Once the last twin has been sewn through, pick up five As. Sew down through the other hole of the twin. Strengthen the ring by sewing up through the twin, back through the five As, and down through the twin. End by following the thread path through the beads, tying several overhand knots along the way. Trim the thread.

25. Repeat step 24 with the other needle.

26. Open a jump ring with two pairs of pliers. Slip one end through the ring of five As at the end of the rope and half of the toggle clasp. Close the jump ring. Repeat for the other end of the rope with the second half of the toggle.

d

e

f

Seeing Double Pendant

Herringbone stitch can be worked flat, in a tube, or, as this design illustrates, in a circle. The radiating herringbone arms create spaces for other beads to sit—perfect for twin beads. Get double usage out of this pendant by stitching it in a second color to make it reversible. Attach a purchased chain, and you have an attractive necklace.

Materials

35 Czech twin beads (opaque mauve pearl terra dyed)

14 Tila beads (dark purple opaque AB)

11º Japanese seed beads
2g in each of **2** colors (lavender galvanized frost and amethyst galvanized metallic)

1g 15º rocailles (fancy rainbow purple)

Finished diameter
2 in. (5cm)

---

1. To make the first circle, cut 48 in. (1.2m) of beading thread, and attach a needle to one end.

Round 1: Using one color of 11º seed bead, pick up an 11º and a 15º seed bead seven times. Sew through all of the beads again to make a snug ring with the beads. Tie the thread ends into a square knot, leaving a 2-in. (5cm) tail. Sew through the first 11º again **(figure 1, a–b)**.

Round 2: Pick up two 11ºs, and sew through the next 11º on the ring. Repeat six times. Step up to the next round by sewing through the first 11º picked up in this round **(figure 1, b–c)**.

Round 3: Pick up two 11ºs. Sew down through the 11º in the round below and up through the next 11º. Repeat six times. Step up to the next round **(c–d)**. End the tail thread at this point, since it will become difficult to do when more rounds have been worked.

Round 4: Pick up two 11ºs, sew down through the 11º in the round below, pick up a 15º, and sew up through the next 11º. Repeat six times. Step up to the next round **(d–e)**.

Round 5: Pick up two 11ºs, sew down through the 11º in the round below, pick up a twin bead, and sew up through the next 11º. Repeat six times. Step up to the next round **(e–f)**.

Round 6: Pick up two 11ºs, and sew down through the 11º in the round below. Pick up a 15º, sew through the second hole of the twin, and pick up a 15º. Sew up through the next 11º. Repeat six more times. Step up to the next round **(f–g)**.

Round 7: Pick up an 11º, a twin, and an 11º, and sew down through the 11º in the round below **(figure 2, a–b)**. Pick up two 15ºs, a Tila bead, and three twins. Sew through the second hole of the Tila **(b–c)**. Sew back up through the Tila. Pick up a 15º, and sew down through the second hole of the Tila. Pick up two 15ºs, and sew up through the next 11º in the round below **(c–d)**. Repeat a–d six times **(d–e)**. To end, follow the thread path through the beads, tying several overhand knots along the way. Trim the thread.

2. Make a second circle: Cut 48 in. (1.2m) of beading thread, and attach a needle to one end. Use the second color of 11ºs. At the beginning of round 5, hold the first half of the pendant behind the current work. Don't pick up any new twins, but sew back through the ones used in the first half. The twins in round 7 are also shared. End the thread as before.

3. Slip a purchased chain between any two Tilas along the outside round of the pendant.

Options

Make this pendant with six sides and use it as a Christmas snowflake decoration.

⬭ Czech twin bead

▮ Tila bead

▢ 11º seed bead

● 15º rocaille

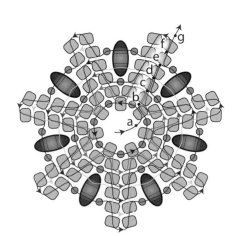

Figure 1

Figure 2

Midnight Sky Necklace

For many years my husband and I have been part of a Lapidary Guild. (As a musician, I like to say I'm part of a Rock Group!) I've learned to cut and polish my own lovely cabochons. I have set them many times using seed beads, but how would it work with these new twins beads? This is one way of setting the stone without first mounting it on some fabric.

Materials

25x20mm oval cabochon
(snowflake obsidian)

20mm round cabochon (snowflake
obsidian)

6 6mm round beads (snowflake
obsidian)

8g Czech twin or SuperDuo beads
(black)

5g 11º Toho seed beads (matte
black)

6g 15º rocailles (shiny black)

2 18-gauge 5mm jump rings (silver)

11mm lobster claw clasp

Finished length
Chain 17½ in. (44cm)
Pendant 2 in. (5cm)

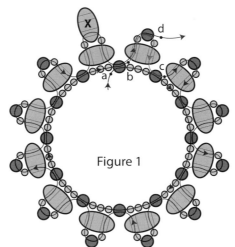

Figure 1

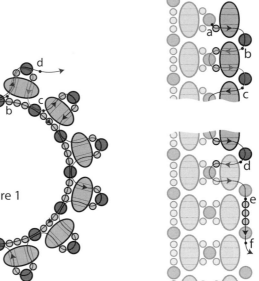

Figure 2

 Czech twin bead

 11º seed bead

 15º rocaille

 6mm round bead

**Because the oval stone is
free to move inside the
beaded bezel, you can wear
it horizontally or vertically.**

Round Cabochon Bezel

1. Cut 40 in. (1m) of thread. Attach a needle to one end and a stop bead 6 in. (15cm) from the other end. Pick up an 11º seed bead and three 15º seed beads 12 times. Sew through all of the beads again plus the first 11º **(figure 1, a–b)**.

2. Pick up a twin bead, a 15º, an 11º, and a 15º. Sew through the second hole of the twin and then the next 11º on the ring **(b–c)**. Repeat 10 times. On the last repeat, substitute a twin for the 11º **(point x)**. This twin will become the bead that joins the round cabochon to the oval cabochon. Follow the thread path through the first twin, 15º, and 11º, exiting the 11º

(c–d). This completes the front half of the bezel.

3. Begin the back half (for clarity, the drawing shows the edge of the bezel): Pick up a 15º, a twin, and an 11º **(figure 2, a–b)**. Pick up a twin and a 15º. Sew through the next 11º along the outside edge of the front bezel. Pick up a 15º, and sew through the second hole of the twin. Pick up an 11º **(b–c)**. Repeat 11 times **(c–d)**. Sew through the unused hole of the first twin added, pick up a 15º, and follow the thread path through the next 11º, 15º, twin, and 11º, exiting the 11º **(d–e)**.

4. Pick up three 15ºs. Sew through the next 11º sitting under the twin **(e–f)**. Repeat 11 times, keeping the thread fairly loose. Place the round cabochon into the bezel, face down. Tighten the thread ring. Pass through all of the beads in the ring again. To finish, follow any thread path through the work, tying several overhand knots along the way. Trim the thread.

Oval Cabochon Bezel

5. Cut 48 in. (1.2m) of thread. Attach a needle to one end and a stop bead 6 in. (15cm) from the other end. Pick up an 11º and three

15ºs 14 times. Sew through all of the beads again plus the first 11º **(figure 3, a–b)**.

6. Pick up a twin, a 15º, an 11º, and a 15º. Sew through the second hole of the twin and then the next 11º on the ring **(b–c)**. Repeat four times. On the fifth repeat, use the A protruding from the outside of the round cabochon bezel instead of picking up an 11º **(point x)**. Repeat b–c eight

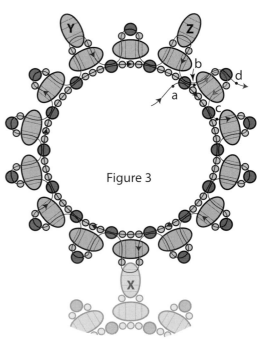

Figure 3

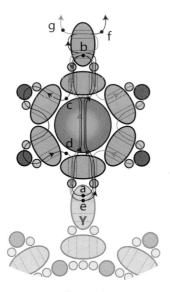

Figure 4

Figure 5

through each of the twin's two holes in the opposite direction of the first needle **(c–d)**.

14. With one needle pick up a 15º, an 11º, a 15º, and a twin. Sew through the second hole of the twin **(d–e)**. With the other needle, pick up a 15º, an 11º, and a 15º. Sew through the two holes of the twin in the opposite direction of the first needle **(b–f)**. Repeat d–e and b–f two more times.

15. Repeat steps 13 and 14 until you reach half of the desired length. End with step 13.

16. To make a loop for the jump rings that attach the clasp, pick up eight 15ºs with one needle. Sew through all of the 15ºs again in the opposite direction with the second needle. Gently pull on the two thread ends until the beads sit snugly together. Tie a square knot. Follow the thread path back through the work with each needle, tying a few half-hitch knots along the way to secure. Trim the thread.

17. To make the second half of the chain, repeat steps 8–16, attaching it to the unused hole of the second twin protruding from the edge of the oval bezel.

18. To attach the lobster claw clasp, open one jump ring using two pairs of pliers. Insert it into the loop of beads at the end of the chain as well as the loop on the clasp. Close the jump ring. Open the second jump ring and attach it to the loop of beads and clasp at the end of the other chain.

more times, substituting a twin for the 11º in the sixth and eighth repeats **(points y and z)**. End by following the thread path through the first twin, 15º, and 11º, exiting the 11º **(c–d)**. This completes the front half of the bezel.

7. To make the back half of the bezel, repeat steps 3 and 4, inserting the oval cabochon face-down into the ring.

Chain

8. Cut 48 in. (1.2m) of thread, and attach a needle to each end. Sew through the unused hole of a twin protruding from the edge of the oval bezel, and center the thread.

9. With one needle, pick up a 15º, a twin, a 6mm round bead, a twin, a 15º, and a twin **(figure 4, a–b, purple)**. With the other needle, pick up a 15º, and sew through the second hole of the first twin picked up, the round, and the second hole of the next twin. Pick up a 15º, and cross the threads through the last twin picked up **(figure 4, a–b, pink)**. Gently pull on both threads at once to make sure all the beads are sitting snugly together.

10. With one needle, follow the thread path back through the 15º and the next twin **(b–c)**. Pick up a twin, a 15º, an 11º, and a 15º. Sew through the second hole of the twin. Repeat, making sure the beads sit together snugly **(c–d)**. Sew through the first hole of the twin already attached, the next 15º and twin on the cabochon bezel **(d–e)**. Follow the thread path back through the 15º, twin, round, twin, 15º, and twin. Sew through the second hole of the twin **(e–f)**.

11. Repeat step 10 with the other thread **(b–g, green)**.

12. Repeat steps 9 and 10 twice to make a total of three snowflake motifs around the rounds.

13. Continue the chain: With one needle, pick up a 15º, an 11º, a 15º, four 11ºs, a 15º, an 11º, a 15º, and a twin. Sew through the second hole of the twin **(figure 5, a–b)**. With the second needle, pick up a 15º, an 11º, and a 15º. Sew through the four 11ºs picked up with the first needle. Pick up a 15º, an 11º, and a 15º. Sew

Options

Substitute any cabochons of the same size (stone, acrylic, ceramic, or glass, for example) for the ones listed here. Choose matching twin beads and seed beads.

80

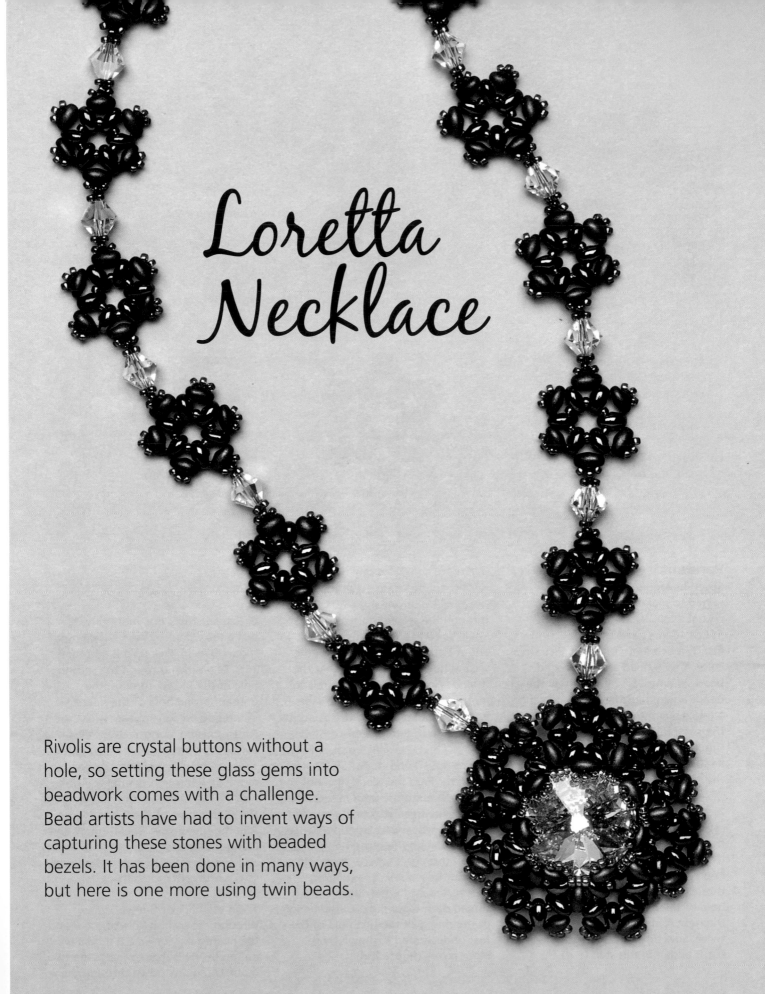

Loretta Necklace

Rivolis are crystal buttons without a hole, so setting these glass gems into beadwork comes with a challenge. Bead artists have had to invent ways of capturing these stones with beaded bezels. It has been done in many ways, but here is one more using twin beads.

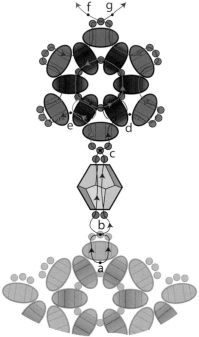

Figure 7

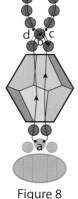

Figure 8

Chain

The hexagonal floral motifs used as a frame for the crystal rivoli are now stitched with two needles to make the chain of the necklace.

10. Cut 80 in. (2m) of thread, and attach a needle to each end. The attachment point is the central B along the free edge of one floral motif on the pendant. With each needle, sew up through the two holes of this center B, plus one 15º. Center the thread, and then cross the thread through the remaining 15º on the edge of the motif **(figure 7, a–b)**.

11. With one needle, pick up a 15º, a 6mm bicone crystal, and two 15ºs. With the second needle, pick up a 15º, sew through the crystal on the first thread, pick up a 15º, and cross the thread through the last 15º on the first thread **(b–c)**.

12. With one needle pick up a 15º, a B, and an A. Sew through the second hole of the A. Pick up a 15º and an A five times, plus one more 15º. Sew through the first A again to form a ring. Sew through the second hole of the A **(c–d)**. With the second needle, pick up a 15º. Sew through the

unused hole of the B and the A next to it. Sew through the second hole of the A, around the ring of As and 15ºs, back through the same hole of the A, and then through the second hole of the same A **(c–e)**.

13. With one needle, pick up a B and three 15ºs. Sew through the second hole of the B and then through the unused hole of the A in the ring below. Repeat. Pick up a B and two 15ºs **(d–f)**. With the second needle, repeat d-f, crossing through the last 15º picked up by the other needle **(e–g)**. Gently pull on both threads at once to make sure the beads sit snugly together.

14. Repeat steps 11–13 seven times for a total of eight crystals alternating with eight floral motifs.

15. Repeat step 11 **(figure 8, a–b)**.

16. To add a loop for the jump ring, pick up eight 15ºs. Sew through all eight 15ºs again **(b–c)**. With the second thread, sew through all eight 15ºs but in the opposite direction to the first thread **(b–d)**. Follow the

thread paths back through the work until each thread is exiting a 15º just above the crystal. Tie the two threads in a square knot, and sew through the crystal. Secure each thread by following the thread paths back through the work, tying a few half-hitch knots along the way. Trim.

17. Make a second chain on an adjacent floral motif around the crystal rivoli.

18. Attach the clasp: Open a jump ring using two pliers and slip it through the loop at the end of one chain. Add one side of the toggle clasp and close the ring. Repeat for the other side.

Options

The necklace chain would make a lovely bracelet. A smaller section of the chain would make attractive earrings.

Once In a Blue Moon Necklace

It is fascinating to see what can be made from polishing the most humble-looking piece of rock. A stone that has a rounded, polished top and a flat, often unpolished back, is called a cabochon. In this project you will learn to stitch around a cab after mounting it on some fabric.

Materials

30x40mm cabochon (turquoise)
23 8mm round beads (turquoise)
Czech twin beads
   15g color A (crystal chrome)
   3g color B (transparent crystal
   rainbow)
3g 11º cylinder beads (transparent
   crystal rainbow or silver-lined
   crystal)
1g 15º Japanese seed beads (steel)
1g 15º rocailles (transparent
   silver-lined silver)
4 in. (10cm) curb chain (silver)
6mm 18-gauge jump ring (silver)
5x10mm lobster claw clasp (silver)
2 4x3 in. (10x8cm) pieces of
   Ultrasuede
waxed cotton quilting thread
   (light gray)

Tools

sharp lead pencil
glue, such as E-6000 adhesive

Finished length
adjustable 19¼–23¼ in (49–59cm)

 Czech twin bead color A

 Czech twin bead color B

 11º seed bead

   ●   15º seed bead

 15º rocaille

 8mm round bead

Figure 1

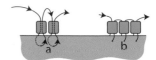

Figure 2

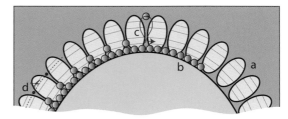

Figure 3

Necklace

First, you will learn two stitches needed in this project: beaded backstitch and beaded blanket stitch.

Beaded Backstitch

a. Thread a needle with a length of quilting thread. Come up into the fabric from behind, leaving a 4-in. (10cm) tail. Pick up four beads. Lay the beads in a snug row. Sew down to the back of the fabric at the end of this row. Come back up near to where you began, without piercing the thread, and sew through all four beads again **(figure 1, a–b)**.

b. Pick up four beads. Lay them in a snug row. Sew down to the back of the fabric at the end of this row. Come up between the second and third beads stitched down in the last step. Sew through the next six beads **(b–c)**. Repeat this "pick up four, go back six" pattern **(c–d)**.

Beaded Blanket Stitch

c. Thread a needle with a length of quilting thread. Pick up a bead. Sew through the fabric, from back to front, 1–1.5mm away from the edge. Sew through the bead in the opposite direction. Pick up a second bead. Sew through the fabric, from back to front, a bead's width away from the first stitch and 1–1.5mm away from the edge. Sew through the bead in the opposite direction **(figure 2, point a)**. Repeat as needed. The beads will sit along the edge with their holes at right angles to the edge of the fabric and a thread bridge running across the tops of the beads **(point b)**.

> **I use cotton quilting thread when working with beads and Ultrasuede. Braided filament thread cuts into the fabric.**

Pendant

1. Glue the cabochon to the center of one of the pieces of Ultrasuede. Let it dry.

2. Thread a needle with a long length of waxed quilting thread. Use a "pick up four, go back six" beaded back-stitch to sew a row of color B twin beads around the cabochon. Use one hole only. The beads should fan out from the cab like the petals on a sunflower **(figure 3, point a)**. Sew through the entire round of Bs again

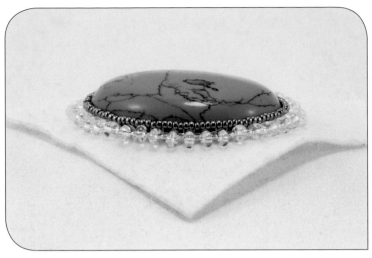

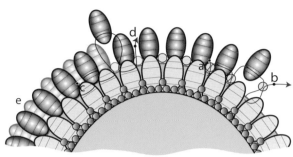

Figure 4

twice. The example uses 37 Bs. Since the size of each cab varies slightly, this number may change for your design. The last few Bs in the round may need to be spaced slightly further apart to make them fit. It is better to use one less bead and increase the space between them slightly, than to squeeze them together and make the row pucker. To end, sew down from any B to the back of the fabric. Come up ½ in. (1cm) away from where you went down, between the row of Bs and the cab.

3. Use a "pick up four, go back two" beaded backstitch to sew a row of 15º seed beads around the cab over the top of the first row of Bs **(point b and photo)**. Sew through the entire round of 15º seeds at least once more, twice if possible. Sew down into the back of the fabric. Come up ½ in. away from where you went down, between any two Bs, near the thread from the first round but without piercing it.

4. Sew through the first hole of the nearest B. Pick up a 15º seed. Sew through the first hole of the next B in the round **(point c)**. Repeat until you have completed the round. Sew through the first B of this round again

and then down to the back of the fabric. To end the thread, weave through several of the thread bridges at the back of the work, tying several overhand knots along the way. Leave a 1-in. (2.5cm) tail, and trim the thread.

5. Use a pencil to make a small mark between each B at the second unused hole. Trim the Ultrasuede at these marks, taking care not to cut any of the threads on the underside **(point d)**. Gently lift the Bs out of the way as you cut.

6. Glue the trimmed cabochon to the second piece of Ultrasuede. Once the glue is dry, carefully trim the second piece to the same size as the first.

7. This round will use a variation of the beaded blanket stitch edge: Thread a needle with a long length of waxed quilting thread. Stitch an 11º seed bead onto the cut edge of the fabric between any two Bs of the first round. Pick up a color A twin bead between each 11º **(figure 4, a–b)**. Repeat a–b around the edge. Some of the thread bridge may show but it will not be visible from the front of

the piece. Finish the round by following the thread path through the first C used and the next A, 11º, and A. End with the thread exiting the closest B of the first round.

8. Pick up a B. Sew through the next A in the round **(c–d)**. Repeat until the thread passes through the first B picked up again. There should be two rows of Bs, one in front of the other, with the beads of the front row sitting between the ones of the back row **(point e)**. Sew through the closest B of the back row, then the next B of the front row. Continue zigzagging between the Bs of the front and back rows until the thread meets the start of the round. Follow the thread path for several centimetres through the beads, tying several overhand knots along the way. Trim the thread.

Chain
9. Cut 28 in. (70cm) of thread, and attach a needle to each end. Decide where the two ropes will be attached to the beaded cabochon (along the back row of As). Sew through the first of these two As. With each needle, pick up two 15º rocailles and center the thread.

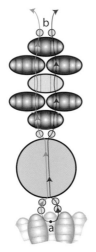

Figure 5

Figure 6

Figure 7

10. With one needle, pick up an 8mm round bead, a rocaille, two As, a B, two As, and a rocaille. With the second needle, sew through the round. Pick up a rocaille, and sew through the second hole of the first A. Pick up an A, and sew through the second hole of the B. Pick up an A, and sew through the second hole of the last A. Pick up a rocaille **(figure 5, a–b)**.

11. Repeat step 10 ten more times, for a total of 11 repeats (or until the rope is the desired length).

12. Make the clasp loop: With one needle, pick up seven rocailles. With the other needle, sew through all seven rocailles in the opposite direction of the first **(figure 6)**. With each needle, follow the thread path back through five twins and a rocaille. Tie the two threads together into a square knot. Follow the thread paths through the work, tying several overhand knots along the way. Trim the thread.

13. Make another rope on the second chosen attachment point.

14. Open the jump ring using two pairs of pliers. Insert it into the loop of seven rocailles on one rope. Add the lobster claw clasp, and close the jump ring.

15. Open the link at the end of the length of chain using two pairs of pliers. Insert it into the loop of seven rocailles on the other rope. Close the link.

Make a Dangle

16. To create a dangle for the extender chain, cut 6 in. (15cm) of beading thread, and attach a needle to one end. Pick up an A and seven rocailles. Sew through the second hole of the A **(figure 8, a–b)**. Pick up a rocaille, a round, and three rocailles. Sew back through the round. Pick up a rocaille **(b–c)**. Sew through the first hole used of the A, all seven rocailles, and the second hole of the A. Tie the two thread ends together in a square knot under the A. Follow the thread path through the beads with each thread end, tying several overhand knots along the way. Trim the thread.

17. Open the last link on the free end of the extender chain using two pairs of pliers. Insert it into the loop of seven Es on the dangle. Close the link.

Specialty Jewelry

Andante Necklace

I find making beads from beads fascinating. They are three-dimensional puzzles in which small geometric shapes are somehow stitched together to make a larger geometric shape. In this project, I challenged myself to make such a bead from SuperDuos and as few other beads as possible.

Materials

20 6–8mm pearls (golden-yellow)
30 6mm pressed glass bicones
    (topaz)
9 6mm beads, any material,
    any color
20g SuperDuos (yellow Picasso)
1g 15º one-cut charlottes
    (metallic gold)
2 18-gauge 5mm jump rings
    (gold-plated)
8–10mm lobster claw clasp
    (gold-plated)
nail polish or permanent marker,
    yellow or green

Finished length
19¼ in. (49cm)

 SuperDuo bead

◉   15º seed bead

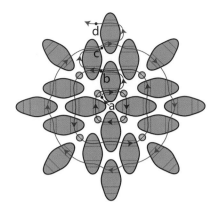

Figure 1

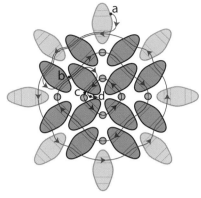

Figure 2

1. If the 6mm beads you have chosen do not match the SuperDuos, color them with permanent marker or nail polish. Cut 16 in. (40cm) of thread, and attach a needle to one end.
Round 1: Pick up a SuperDuo and a 15º seed bead four times. Sew through all of the beads again. Tie the two ends into a secure square knot, leaving a 3-in. (7.5cm) tail. Sew through the first SuperDuo again. Sew through the second hole of the same SuperDuo so the thread changes direction **(figure 1, a–b)**.
Round 2: Pick up a SuperDuo, a 15º, and a SuperDuo. Sew through the second hole of the next SuperDuo. Repeat three times. Sew through the first SuperDuo picked up again. Sew through the second hole of the same SuperDuo **(b–c)**.
Round 3: Pick up a SuperDuo, and sew through the next SuperDuo of the round below. Repeat seven times. Sew through the first SuperDuo picked up

again. Sew through the second hole of the same SuperDuo **(c–d)**.
Round 4: Repeat round 3 but at the end of the round, sew through the first four SuperDuos again. Sew through the second hole of the same A **(figure 2, a–b)**.
Round 5: Pick up a SuperDuo. Sew through the next SuperDuo in the round below. Pick up a 15º. Sew through the next SuperDuo in the round below. Repeat three times. Sew through the first SuperDuo picked up again. Sew through the second hole of the same SuperDuo **(b–c)**. Insert a 6mm bead inside the shape made so far. Insert a sewing pin or needle into the first round and through the inner bead so you don't lose the location of the hole.
Round 6: Pick up a 15º, and sew through the next SuperDuo. Repeat three more times, then sew through all of the beads twice.

3. End by following the thread path back through the work, tying several overhand knots along the way. Repeat for the tail end.

4. Make a total of nine beaded beads.

> **Since each bead uses only 32 SuperDuos, this project is a great way to use up leftover beads.**

5. String the necklace: Cut 36 in. (90cm) of thread, and attach a needle to one end. Pick up a beaded bead, and center it on the thread. Add a stop bead to the tail and push it up against the beaded bead.

6. Pick up a bicone crystal, a pearl, a crystal, and a beaded bead. Repeat three times. Pick up an alternating pattern of a crystal and a pearl until you have used six pearls, ending with a crystal. Pick up 10 15ºs. Sew through all of the 15ºs again. Tie the working thread and main thread into a square knot under the ring of 15ºs. Sew back through the strand of beads, tying several overhand knots along the way, to end the tail.

7. Undo the stop bead and repeat step 6 with the other half of the thread.

8. Open a jump ring with two pairs of pliers. Insert one end into the loop of 15ºs and the lobster claw clasp. Close the jump ring. Open the second jump ring. Insert it into the other loop of 15ºs and close the ring.

Options

A pair of these beads on headpins makes lovely earrings.

Candy Chain Necklace and Bracelet

When I first started designing with twin beads, I found that they make very nice curves if you pick several up through one hole and stitch a single bead between each through the second hole. When you change sides partway along, they make a wonderful S-shape. Interlock the S-shapes for a piece full of movement and flair.

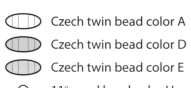

- ⬭ Czech twin bead color A
- ⬭ Czech twin bead color D
- ⬭ Czech twin bead color E
- ○ 11º seed bead color H
- ◐ 11º seed bead color K
- ◑ 11º seed bead color L

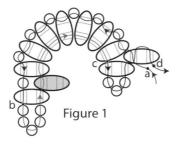

Figure 1

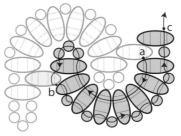

Figure 2

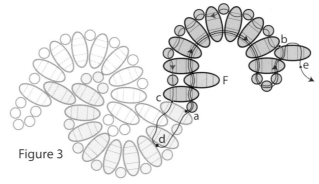

Figure 3

Materials

Necklace

5g Czech twin or SuperDuo beads in each of **6** colors: A–F (yellow, dark pink, pink, green, aqua, and violet solgel)

2g 11º Czech seed beads in each of **6** colors: H–M (yellow, dark pink, pink, green, aqua, violet)

2 20-gauge 5mm jump rings, (silver-plated)

toggle clasp, silver-plated

Bracelet

2g Czech twin seed beads in each of the colors above, plus color G (gray solgel)

1g 11º Czech seed beads in each of the colors above, plus color N (gray)

2 20-gauge 5mm jump rings (silver plated)

clasp

Finished length

Necklace 19¼ in. (49cm)

Bracelet 7 in. (17.5cm)

Necklace

1. Cut a long length of thread. Attach a needle to one end and a stop bead to the other, leaving a 4-in. (10cm) tail.

2. Pick up two color A twin beads. Pick up a color H 11º seed bead and an A seven times (**figure 1, a–b**). Pick up five Hs and sew through the second hole of the last A picked up. Pick up a color D twin bead, and sew through the second hole of the next seven As (**b–c**). Pick up an A and three Hs. Sew through the second hole of the last A picked up (**c–a**). Undo the stop bead, and tie the two threads together securely into a square knot. Sew through the first A picked up and the second hole of the same A (**a–d**).

3. Pick up eight Ds and three color K 11º seed beads. Sew through the second hole of the D and the second hole of the D added in step 2 (**figure 2, a–b**). Sew through the second hole of the next D, and pick up a D. Repeat six times. Pick up a K (**b–c**).

4. Pick up a K, a D, an E, eight Ds, and three Ks. Sew through the second

hole of the last D picked up, and pick up a D (**figure 3, a–b**). Sew through the second hole of the next D. Pick up a K, and sew through the second hole of the next D seven times (**b–c**). Sew through the next D, A, and D (**c–d**). Turn around by sewing through the second hole of the same D, and on through the next K and D. Follow the thread path through the beads until point b of figure 3. Sew through the second hole of that K (**d–e**). The S-shaped motif will have a bit of a "kink" in it at **point c**. This is so the work will curve and fit the shape of the neck.

Since it is difficult to pass a needle through the tight inside curve, leave a loop of thread at point d (where you will turn around).

Follow the instructions but leave the tension quite loose. Once the needle has reached point b, tighten the work at the loop and pull the remaining thread through.

5. Repeat steps 3 and 4 using twin bead colors E, F, C, and B next, in that order. Remember that the bead at **figure 3, point F** is always the color to be worked next. Repeat the entire sequence of six colors four times, ending with step 3 using As.

6. To finish, pick up five Hs and sew through the second hole of the A the thread is leaving plus the B below it. Follow the thread path through the inner curve of beads, and then around the outside edge, tying several over-hand knots along the way. Trim the thread. Finish off the tail end at the start of the work in the same way.

7. To add the clasp, open a jump ring. Insert it through the loop on one half of the clasp plus the loop of seed beads on one end of the work. Close the jump ring. Repeat with the second half of the clasp on the other end of the necklace.

> **It is not easy to sew through the inner curve made by the twin beads sitting together and your needle will probably bend. Don't throw it away; it will probably navigate the corners better now!**

Bracelet

1. Repeat steps 1–4 of "Necklace," except in step 4, add an 11º seed bead at point c. This prevents the "kink" and allows the bracelet to lay straight. The colors used are B (half an S-shape), G, C, A, D, E, F, and B (the other half of the S-shape).

2. Add a clasp as in the necklace.

Options

Make a stately version of this necklace with only two colors of twin beads. This two-tone version uses contrasting light and dark hues.

Oriana Necklace

I really like the look of beadwork combined with a few metal links and jump rings. These fan motifs seemed to go perfectly between the swirls of metal.

Materials

16 8mm round beads (fossil ivory
   or cream)
15g Czech SuperDuo beads (fire
   opal picasso)
2g 10º Japanese cylinder beads
   (green iris)
2g 11º Czech seed beads (cream)
2g 15º Japanese cylinder beads
   (matte dark olive)
16 20-gauge 5mm jump rings
   (gold-plated)
8 8x27mm gold links
11x7mm gold-plated lobster clasp

Finished length
22 in. (56cm)

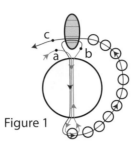

Figure 1

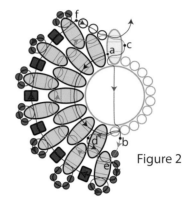

Figure 2

 SuperDuo bead

 8mm round bead

 10º seed bead

 11º seed bead

 15º cylinder bead

**This design is not suitable
for twin beads.**

Necklace

1. Cut 36 in. (90cm) of thread, and
attach a needle to one end. Pick up
an 8mm round bead and an 11º seed
bead, leaving a 6-in. (15cm) tail. Sew
back through the round **(figure 1,
a–b)**, pick up a SuperDuo, and sew
through the round plus the 11º
already there. These two beads sit on
top of the hole through the round
and will be referred to as anchor
SuperDuo and anchor 11º. Pick up 10
more 11ºs, and sew through the
anchor SuperDuo using the same hole
(b–c). Make sure the beads sit snugly
together. Tie a square knot with the
working thread and tail. Undo the
needle, and attach it to the tail
thread. Finish off the tail by following
the thread path through the beads. It
will be virtually impossible to do this

later. Re-attach the needle to the
working thread.

2. Pick up seven SuperDuos. Sew
through the anchor 11º **(figure 2, a–b)**.

3. Pick up a 15º cylinder bead and a
SuperDuo. Sew through the second
hole of the last SuperDuo just added,
changing direction. Pick up a Super-
Duo, and sew through the second
hole of the next SuperDuo in the
round below. Repeat five times for a
total of seven SuperDuos added in
this row. Pick up an 11º, and sew
through the second hole of the
anchor SuperDuo **(b–c)**. Sew through
the first hole of the anchor SuperDuo,
the round, the anchor 11º, and the
SuperDuo next to it **(c–d)**. Change

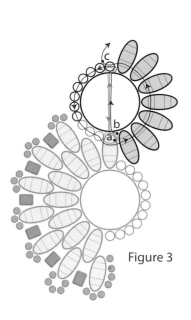

Figure 3

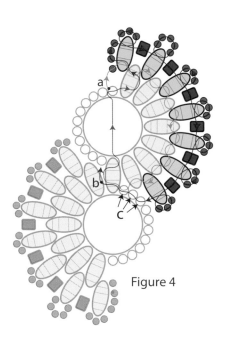

Figure 4

Figure 5

direction by sewing through the second hole of the same SuperDuo and following the thread path through the next SuperDuo **(d–e)**.

4. Start the edge embellishment: Pick up three 15º s, sew through the second hole of the SuperDuo, pick up three 15º s, and sew through the same hole again. Pick up a 10º seed bead, sew through the second hole of the next SuperDuo in the round, pick up five 15º s, and sew through the same SuperDuo. This is the only edge picot using five 15º s, and it will become the loop to insert a jump ring when joining the motifs together. Pick up a 10º, and sew through the second hole of the next SuperDuo in the round. Continue along the row in the same

manner, sewing three 15º s over every SuperDuo and a 10º between each SuperDuo **(e–f)**. Pick up two 11º s, and sew through the 11º in the row below plus the second hole of the anchor SuperDuo, exiting at point c.

5. Begin the second half of the fan motif: Pick up a round and an 11º, and sew back through the round and anchor SuperDuo. Sew back through the round and the 11º, which is the new anchor 11º. Pick up seven 11º s. Sew through the three 11º s from the first half, plus the anchor SuperDuo. Pick up seven SuperDuos, and sew through the new anchor 11º **(figure 3, a–b)**.

6. Repeat steps 3 and 4 **(figure 4, a–b)**. Do not pick up any new 11º s, but use the three next to the anchor 11º already in the ring around the round **(point c)**. To finish, follow any thread

path through the work, tying several overhand knots along the way to secure. Trim both the working and tail threads.

7. Repeat steps 1–6 five times to make a total of six two-fan motifs.

8. The motif at the center has three fans; make the first one by repeating steps 1–4. Make the second by repeating step 5 with the following changes in the first round: Use an anchor SuperDuo in place of the second anchor 11º, pick up seven SuperDuos between the two anchor SuperDuos, and use nine 11º s on the other side (three from the first fan). This affects the second row. Pick up six SuperDuos to sit between the first row of SuperDuos **(figure 5, b beads)**. Embellish only the tops of the SuperDuos with 10º s in between. You may need to add an extra 10º in the places marked a **(figure 5)**. The third fan is made by repeating steps 5 and 6. It faces the same direction as the first fan.

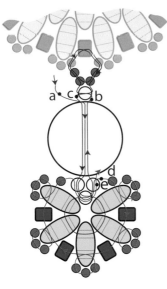

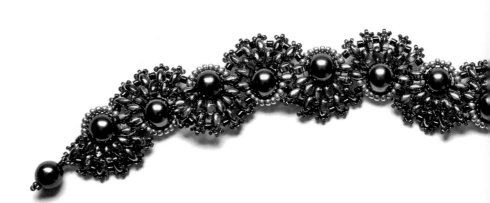

Figure 6

9. Make a dangle: Cut 12 in. (30cm) of thread, and add a needle to one end. Pick up a round, two 11°s and five SuperDuos, leaving a 4-in. (10cm) tail. Sew through the last 11° picked up, in the same direction, forming a ring of SuperDuos. Pick up an 11°, and sew back through the round **(figure 6, a–b)**. Pick up an 11° and two 15°s. Sew through the 15°, 10°, and 15° at the lower center front edge of the three-fan motif. Pick up two 15°s. Sew through all the 15°s and 10° again to tighten the loop. Sew through the 11° in the opposite direction **(b–c)**. Sew through the round and three 11°s picked up at the start **(c–d)**. Pick up a 15°, and sew through the second hole of the nearest SuperDuo. Pick up three 15°s, sew through the same SuperDuo again, pick up a 10°, and sew through the second hole of the next SuperDuo. Repeat three times. Pick up three 15°s, and sew through the SuperDuo again. Pick up a 15°. Sew through all three 11°s at the base

of the round **(d–e)**. Finish off by following the thread path through the work, tying several overhand knots along the way. Trim the thread. Finish off the tail end.

Assembly
10. Open all of the jump rings. Insert a jump ring into one end of a link and the five-bead loop of 15°s on the three–fan motif. Close the jump ring. Insert a second jump ring into the other end of the link and the five-bead loop of 15°s on one of the two-fan motifs. Continue joining motifs and links in an alternating pattern until half of each has been used. Repeat on the other side of the central motif until the remaining links and motifs have been used. End one side of the necklace with only a jump ring, and the other with a jump ring and the lobster claw clasp. To do up the necklace, open the lobster claw clasp and slip it through the last jump ring.

Options

- Give the design a classic look with glass pearls in place of the fossil ivory.
- To decrease the length of the necklace, use shorter links or omit some of the motifs. To make it longer, add some more links and motifs.
- Make a bracelet by joining several fans in a continuous straight line.

Elsie Necklace

When dealing with a broken zipper on my coat, it occurred to me that twin beads look like the teeth of a zipper. Make sure that you stitch the slider firmly in place. Someone is sure to come up to you, wanting to zip up your necklace!

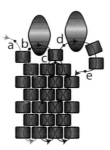

Figure 1

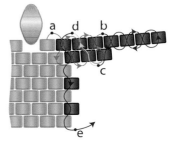

Figure 2

Materials

Tila bead (dark bronze opaque metallic)
11g SuperDuo beads (bronze)
22g 10° cylinder beads (transparent silver-lined burgundy wine)
2g 15° seed beads (burgundy)
slider from a size 5 zipper with metal teeth, gold or bronze
6 20-gauge 5mm jump rings, gold-plated
13x6mm three-strand end bars with lobster claw clasp and extender chain, antiqued brass

Extra tools
small screwdriver

Finished length
Unzipped section 10¼ in. (26cm)
Zipped-up section 3¾ in. (9.5cm)

There is a significant difference in size between an 11° and a 10° cylinder bead. Be sure to use 10°s for this project. Twin beads are not recommended.

Necklace

1. At the top of the fabric zipper are metal tabs that prevent the slider from coming off the end. Pry these tabs off with a small screwdriver and pair of pliers. Remove the zipper slider.

I was able to buy the zipper used in this project for under $4. There are always cast-off zippers in thrift stores, and some fabric stores sell zipper sliders. My zipper has a manufactured pull, but you can make your own from beads to match your project.

2. Cut a long length of thread. Attach a needle to one end and a stop bead 6 in. (15cm) from the other end.

3. Pick up seven 10° cylinder beads. These form the first two rows of peyote stitch. Pick up a 10°, and sew up through the sixth 10°. Pick up a 10°. Skipping a 10° in the previous row, sew up through the next 10°. Pick up a 10°. Skipping a 10° in the previous row, sew up through the next two 10°s **(figure 1, a–b)**. Pick up a SuperDuo and two 10°s. Sew down through the next "out" bead. Finish the row in peyote stitch, adding two beads. Pick up a bead, and sew up through the next "out" bead. Repeat twice, adding three beads to this row. Turn around underneath the bead closest to the SuperDuo **(b–c)**. Pick up a 10°, and sew down through the next "out" bead. Repeat twice, adding three beads to this row. Pick up a 10°, and sew up through the next "out" bead. Repeat. Pick up a 10°, and sew up through the next "out" bead and the 10° above it **(c–d)**. Pick up a SuperDuo and two 10°s. Sew down through the next "out" bead **(d–e)**.

4. Repeat b–d until you have used 58 SuperDuos or the work is the desired length, adding thread as needed. The unique shape of the zipper slider means that the beadwork that goes through it also has a unique shape. You'll make a slight bend to help the zipper hang better.

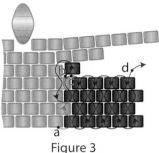

Figure 3

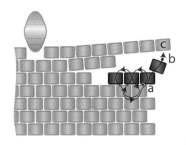

Figure 4

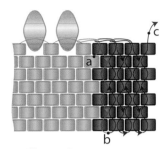

Figure 5

5. End at point d. Pick up a 10º, and sew back through the nearest 10º of the row below. Pick up a 10º and sew back through the first 10º picked up. Repeat to make a two-row section of peyote stitch with six beads **(figure 2, a–b)**. Pick up four 10ºs, sew back through the second-to-last 10º picked up, and continue on to make a four-bead ladder. Sew down through the last "out" bead of the small peyote stitch band just made **(b–c)**. Travel diagonally up through two beads **(c–d)**. Sew down through three beads, and then finish the row in peyote stitch, adding two beads **(d–e)**.

6. Pick up a 10º, and sew through up through the next "out" bead. Repeat **(figure 3, a–b)**. Pick up a 10º. Sew down through three beads and up through two, forming a figure 8 with the thread and coming out under the bead just picked up **(b–c)**. Set aside 16 10ºs on your work surface. Use all of these beads to stitch four horizontal rows of peyote stitch **(c–d)**.

7. Pick up two 10ºs. Sew down through the 10º the thread was leaving, and up through the 10º beside it and the second one added. Pick up a 10º. Sew down through the 10º below. Travel through the 10ºs at the edge of the work, exiting the first 10º picked up. Pick up a 10º **(figure 4, a–b)**. You will notice that the narrow tab along the tooth edge of the work is one row longer than the peyote stitch area below. This will make the necklace bend inside the slider, helping it to hang better.

8. Lay the beaded zipper on your work surface with the SuperDuo "teeth" on the right. Insert the small peyote extension made in step 4 into the left side of the zipper slider. Sew through the bead at the end of the ladder stitches, indicated by point c in figure 4. Pick up a SuperDuo and two 10ºs. Sew through the "out" bead nearest the "teeth" edge of the zipper **(photo a)**. Finish the row in peyote stitch.

9. Resume stitching the zipper, as shown in step 1, b–d, until 15 SuperDuos have been used. End at point d without sewing through the second 10º. Pick up a 10º. Sew under the thread between the SuperDuo and the 10º, and then back down through the 10º just picked up. Finish the row in peyote stitch, picking up three beads **(figure 5, a–b)**. Work five rows in odd-count peyote, sewing under the thread at the top of every second row to turn around **(b–c)**.

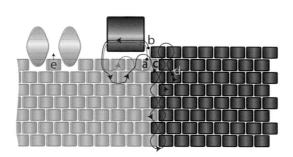

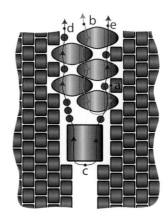

Figure 6

Figure 7

10. Pick up a Tila bead. Sew down into the second 10º away from the last SuperDuo "tooth". Sew up and down through the 10ºs along the edge to exit where the thread left **(figure 6, a–b)**. Sew through the Tila again, to reinforce, down through the same 10º, into the 10º below, up and across a 10º, up again, and down through the 10º where the thread left **(b–c)**. Finish the row in peyote stitch. Turn around and add three 10ºs using peyote stitch. Pick up three 10ºs. Sew back through the third 10º added. Continue the row in peyote stitch. Work more rows of even-count peyote stitch until there are eight beads along the edge after the Tila, ending that horizontal row with an "out" bead. End the thread by following the thread paths back through the work, tying several overhand knots along the way and changing direction at least twice. This is the first side of the zipper completed.

The second side is made just like the first with a couple of minor changes.

The teeth on the closed part of the zipper need to be staggered so that they "zip" up. This is done by adding an extra row of peyote stitch just after the beads are stitched through the slider, and removing a row next to the Tila.

11. Repeat steps 1–7.

12. Lay the first half of the beaded zipper upside down on your work surface. Insert the small peyote extension made in step 5 into the unused side of the zipper slider. Sew through the bead at the end of the ladder stitches, indicated by point c in figure 4. Do not pick up any beads. Sew through two beads below the one the thread is leaving **(photo b)**. Finish the row in peyote stitch. This would be similar to making the regular part of the zipper without adding a SuperDuo "tooth" (refer to figure 1, b–c).

13. Repeat step 9. The first "tooth" being added is shown in **photo c**. Stitch only three rows of odd-count peyote stitch at the end of the step. Refer to figure 5. Repeat step 10. This is the second side completed. If the working thread end is 8 in. (20cm) or longer, use it to continue. Sew through the beads to exit the B between the two As closest to the

Tila, shown as point e in figure 6. If the second thread end is too short, end it and begin a new thread 12 in. (30cm) long to exit in the same place.

14. Sew through the nearest hole of the SuperDuo, toward the Tila, and then through the second hole. Sew through the second hole of the SuperDuo on the other side of the zipper, then the second hole of the next SuperDuo on the first side of the zipper. Continue along **(figure 7, a–b)**, alternating sides, until all 30 Super-Duos have been zipped together. Sew up through the beads inside the slider, then back down along the other side inside the slider. Sew back through 29 SuperDuos, then through the second hole of the 29th SuperDuo. End the thread by following the thread paths back through the work, tying several overhand knots along the way and changing direction at least twice.

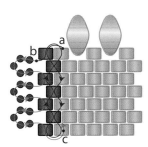

Figure 8

15. Cut 30 in. (80cm) of thread. Attach a needle to one end, and a stop bead half way along. Sew through the left hole of the Tila, heading towards the "teeth". Pick up three 15º seed beads. Sew through the next SuperDuo, using the hole closest to the peyote stitching. Pick up a 15º. Sew through the next A, using the same hole **(c–d)**. Continue along all the way up to the end of the zipper, adding a 15º between each SuperDuo. Do not add any 15ºs inside the slider area. Make sure the tension is loose enough not to create puckers in the zipper. End the thread. Undo the stop bead and attach a needle to the thread. Sew through the right hole of the Tila, heading towards the "teeth". Pick up a 15º. Sew through the next A, using the hole closest to the peyote stitch-ing **(c–e)**. Continue along all the way up the zipper, adding a 15º between each SuperDuo, like the first side. End the thread.

Clasp

16. Undo the stop bead at the start of the necklace. Pick up two 10ºs, and sew down through the next "out" bead. Finish the row in peyote stitch. Turn around and work peyote stitch, adding three beads. Sew through the 10º where the thread first exited and down through the first 10º picked up **(figure 8, a–b)**. Pick up five 15ºs, and sew through the next "out" bead. Repeat twice. Sew up through the next bead **(b–c)**. Follow the thread path through the 15ºs again to strengthen the loops. End the thread.

17. Repeat step 16 on the other end of the necklace. Open all six jump rings. Use three to attach one of the three-strand end bars, matching the beaded loops with the metal loops. Repeat on the other side.

Winter Harvest Necklace

Wheat stitch is unique to two-hole beads. Twins look like grains of wheat and because of the two holes, can be stitched in the V-shape typical of a sheaf of wheat. The delicate fan-shape looks like something icy and wintery in the silver color. I live in Canada, and I was stitching this project when The Great White North was living up to its name.

Materials

19 8mm glass pearls (dark gray)
17g Czech twin beads or SuperDuos
(full Labrador silver)
88 6º Japanese seed beads
(metallic plum iris)
7g 11º Japanese seed beads
(metallic silver)
3g 15º rocailles (transparent
silver-lined silver)
2 20-gauge 5mm jump rings
(silver plated)
13mm silver toggle clasp

Finished length
16½ in. (42cm)

Czech twin bead

6º seed bead

11º seed bead

15º rocaille

8mm glass pearl

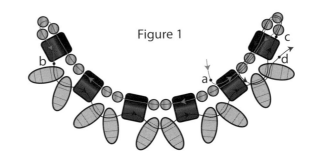

Figure 1

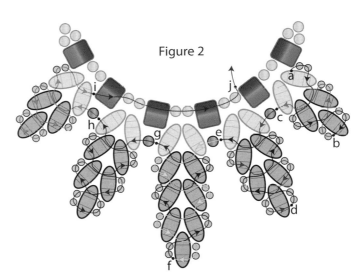

Figure 2

Necklace

1. Begin the fan-shaped components:
Cut 24 in. (60cm) of thread, and
attach a needle to one end. Pick up a
6º seed bead, two 11º seed beads, a
6º, and three 11ºs. Skipping the last
three 11ºs picked up, sew back
through all the beads. Pull gently on
the needle thread until the three 11ºs
sit snugly against the 6º, making a
three-bead picot. Continue to pull the
thread until it leaves a 3-in. (7.5cm)
tail. Pick up two 15º seed beads and a
6º four more times. Pick up three 11ºs,
and sew back through the last 6º
added. Pull the thread until the last
three 11ºs added form a picot against
the last 6º **(figure 1, a–b)**. Pick up two
twin beads, and sew through the next
6º. Repeat four times **(b–c)**. Follow the
thread path back through the first
picot made, the next 6º, and two 11ºs.
Turn around by sewing through the
last two twins added **(c–d)**.

2. Pick up two 15ºs, and sew through
the second hole of the twin. Pick up
two twins and two 15ºs. Sew through
the second hole of the twin just
picked up. Pick up a twin and two

15ºs. Sew through the second hole of
the twin just picked up **(figure 2, a–b)**.
Pick up two 15ºs. Sew through the
twin (so that the thread paths cross)
and the unused hole of the first twin
picked up in this step. Pick up two
15ºs. Sew through the first two twins
picked up plus the second twin of the
previous step **(b–c)**. This completes the
first five-bead wheat sheaf.

3. Pick up an 11º. Sew through the
next twin added in step 1. Pick up two
twins and two 15ºs, then sew through
the second hole of the twin just
picked up. Repeat. Pick up a twin and

two 15ºs. Sew through the second
hole of the twin just picked up **(c–d)**.
Pick up two 15ºs. Sew through the
twin (so that the thread paths cross)
and the unused hole of the closest
twin. Pick up two 15ºs. Sew through
the next two twins so that the thread
paths cross, plus the unused hole of
the closest twin. Pick up two 15ºs. Sew
through the next two twins so that
the thread paths cross, plus the
unused hole in the next twin from
step 1 **(d–e)**. This completes the first
seven-bead wheat sheaf.

105

Gallery

Vine Necklace

Atlantea

Manindra

Lady of the Rings

Venetian
Christmas

Christianne

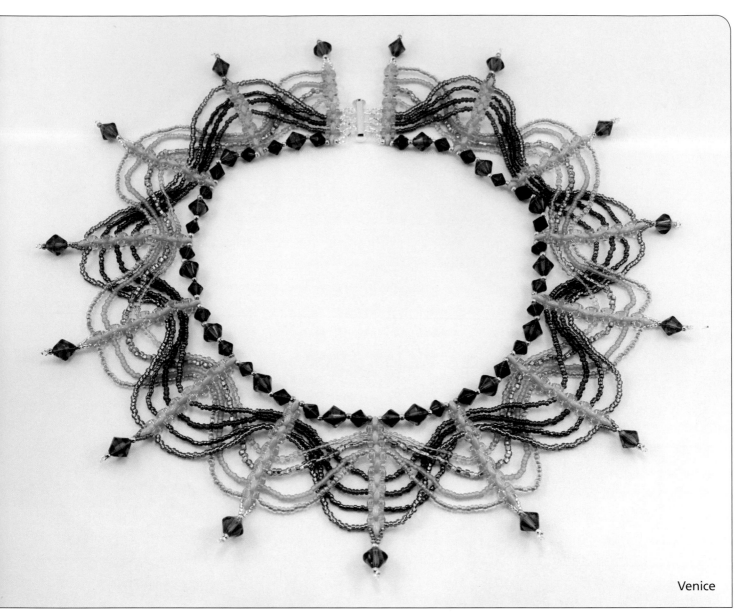

Venice

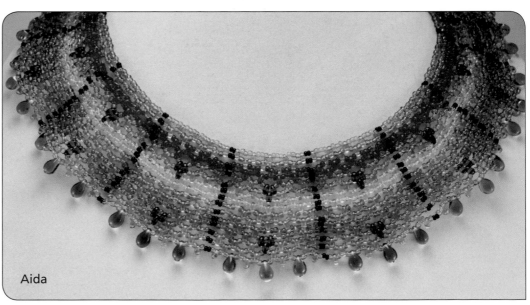

Aida

Acknowledgments

One can never undertake a grand project such as writing a book without acknowledging the help of numerous people. Thank you to:

My husband Tony, for his steady encouragement and constant love.

My daughter Lyndall, for doing her part in ridding the world, and this manuscript, of misplaced apostrophes and superfluous wordage; and for the handy tips using the drawing program.

My daughter Dara, for testing some of the projects, making alternate color examples, and cooking all those good meals.

My daughter Bethany, for being her hilarious self and not getting squished by an aardvark. You keep us in stitches.

My friend Brenda, always enthusiastic and a partner in bead crime. I don't think we are actually criminals, but there must be something illegal about have such fun with beads.

Our enthusiastic friends at Rock Club, who know about things like dopping, benitoite, and grit, and are such fun to be with.

My editor Erica, for sewing this whole book together.

The photographers at Kalmbach, Bill and Jim, for making the projects look stunning in photographs. They are a SuperDuo.

My Heavenly Father, the ultimate Creator, for allowing me this opportunity to create.

Artist Biography

Carolyn Cave

A self-taught bead artist living in Alberta, Carolyn enjoys the endless creativity derived from stringing and stitching "little round shiny things with holes in them." This is both a frustrating and exhilarating way to fill in the spare moments of her very full days as a wife, mother of three young ladies, and musician. Creativity has always played a large role in her life, from sewing clothes for Barbie at a young age, to experimenting with a wide variety of arts and crafts; from earning a Degree in Music and playing several instruments, to making jewelry. Her creations are inspired by a wide variety of things—the colours and shapes of the natural world, works of vintage and antique beaded art, the encouraging comments of her family, and the many hours spent "composing" with needle, beads, and thread. Her work has been published in *Bead&Button* and *Beadwork* magazines, and she has been a winner in multiple categories of BeadStar every year since 2011. This is her first book. You can see some of Carolyn's work on her Facebook page, Lady Beadle Designs.

photo by Bethany Cave

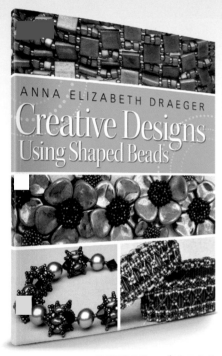